# Hg2 Madrid

A Hedonist's guide to
# Madrid

BY Beverley Fearis
PHOTOGRAPHY Lyndon Douglas & Beverley Fearis

A Hedonist's guide to Madrid

Managing director – Tremayne Carew Pole
Series editor – Catherine Blake
Production – Navigator Guides
Design – P&M Design
Typesetting – Dorchester Typesetting
Repro – PDQ Digital Media Solutions
Printers – Printed in Italy by Printer Trento srl
PR – Ann Scott Associates
Publisher – Filmer Ltd

Email – info@ahedonistsguideto.com
Website – www.ahedonistsguideto.com

First published in the United Kingdom in 2004 by
Filmer Ltd
47 Filmer Road
London SW6 7JJ

ISBN - 0-9547878-1-1

# Hg2 Madrid

## CONTENTS

# How to…

A Hedonist's guide to… is broken down into easy to use sections:
Sleep, Eat, Drink, Snack, Party, Culture, Shop, Play and Info. In each of
these sections you will find detailed reviews and photographs.

At the front of the book there is an introduction to the city and an
overview map, followed by introductions to the four main areas and
more detailed maps. On each of these maps you will see the places
that we have reviewed, laid out by section, highlighted on the map with
a symbol and a number. To find out about a particular place, simply
turn to the relevant section where all entries are listed alphabetically.

Alternatively, browse through a specific section (i.e. Eat) until you find
a restaurant that you like the look of. Next to your choice will be a
small coloured dot – each colour refers to a particular area of the city
– then simply turn to the relevant map to discover the location.

# Updates

Due to the lengthy publishing process and shelf lives of books it is
very difficult to keep travel guides up to date – new restaurants, bars
and hotels open up all the time, while others simply fade away or just
go out of style. What we can offer you are free updates – simply log
onto our website www.ahedonistsguideto.com and enter your details,
answer a relevant question to provide proof of purchase and you will
be entitled to free updates for a year from the date that you sign up.
This will enable you to have all the relevant information at your finger
tips whenever you go away.

In order to help us with this any comments that you might have, or
recommendations that you would like to see in the guide in future
please feel free to email us at info@ahedonistsguideto.com.

# The concept

A Hedonist's guide to… is designed to appeal to a more urbane and stylish traveller. The kind of traveller who is interested in gourmet food, elegant hotels and seriously chic bars – the traveller who feels the need to explore, shop and pamper themselves away from the madding crowd.

Our aim is to give you the inside knowledge of the city, to make you feel like a well-heeled, sophisticated local and to take you to the most fashionable places in town to rub shoulders with the local glitterati.

In today's world work rules our life, weekends away are few and far between, and when we do go away we want to have the most fun and relaxation possible with the minimum of stress. This guide is all about maximizing time. Everywhere is photographed, so before you go you know exactly what you are getting into; choose a restaurant or bar that suits you and your demands.

We pride ourselves on our independence and our integrity. We eat in all the restaurants, drink in all the bars and go wild in the nightclubs – all totally incognito. We charge no one for the privilege of appearing in the guide; every place is reviewed and included at our discretion.

We feel cities are best enjoyed by soaking up the atmosphere and the vibrancy; wander the streets, indulge in some retail relaxation therapy, re-energize yourself with a massage and then get ready to eat like a king and party hard on the stylish local scene.

We believe that it is important for you to explore a city on your own terms, while the places reviewed provide definitive coverage in our eyes; one's individuality can never be wholly accounted for. Whatever you do we can assure you that you will have an unforgettable week-end.

# Madrid

It would be hard to find a city that lends itself more readily to the pursuit of hedonism than Madrid. Known as the party capital of Europe, it has a level of vibrancy and energy unparalleled in other cities, and this is largely because of the character of its people.

Visitors will be left wondering when these crazy Madrilenos find time to sleep, or go to work. Indeed, no matter what night of the week, you'll find bars and restaurants bursting with people well into the early hours.

The Madrilenos love to get dressed up, meet with friends, talk, drink, eat and talk some more – at full volume – and such inconsequential things as work and sleep seem to take second place. Even on the rare dull and drizzly days, the locals are still out and about enjoying themselves and making the most of what their city has to offer.

Madrid is the highest, sunniest and greenest capital in Europe and, according to its natives, is the closest place you'll get to heaven – '*Desde Madrid al Cielo*' goes the saying.

It does, of course, have the same problems with traffic and overcrowding as any other major European city, but one of its major selling-points is its small size. Madrid is so compact that even in an afternoon you can cover considerable ground. What's more, the street layout is straightforward and most of the major attractions are within easy reach.

If time allows, however, it's definitely worth exploring the districts that lie beyond the city centre, such as Salamanca, La Latina and Malasana, each with its own distinctive character. In this guide, we've divided the city into four areas: Centro, Chueca and Malasana, The Old City/La Latina and Salamanca, and in a weekend you should be able to experience them all.

As a tourist destination Madrid is underrated and is often overlooked for its coastal rival, Barcelona. It is, however, home to three stunning and important museums and has several beautiful parks to make up for its lack of beaches.

It also offers a far more authentic Spanish experience than Barcelona. Not so much English is spoken (you'll have to brush up on your Spanish vocab or invest in a phrase book), and Spanish traditions, such as long, leisurely lunches and late dinners, are still very much part of everyday life.

Luckily, this means you won't have to rush around in the heat of the day in order to see as much of the city as possible. Temperatures soar into the 30s in the summer and many visitors will find it uncomfortable and exhausting to be out in the midday sun. At the height of the summer temperatures can creep into the 40s and, understandably, many Madrilenos pack up and leave for the latter half of July and throughout August.

At this time, you'll get some great bargains on hotel rooms and the streets will be less crowded, but many of the better restaurants and bars will be closed. With the heat, it's best to take things at an easy pace and to make the most of the fabulous restaurants and cafés that are open. Don't grab snacks on the move. Do as the Madrilenos do and take your time.

This culture of long lunches and lazy, coffee-sipping afternoons means you won't tire yourself out before heading off again for the long night ahead. Once the clock strikes midnight, Europe's ultimate pleasure playground really comes into its own and will keep even the most hardcore party animal entertained until the sun comes up.

EL
VISO

SALAMANCA

ASTELLANA
LISTA

COLETOS

NIMOS

PACIFICO

ATOCHA

## EAT

7. La Broche
15. El Chaflan
34. Santceloni
35. Tao

## PARTY

4. Fortuny
8. Moma
12. Space of Sound
21. Oz Teatro

## CULTURE

1. Casa de Campo
7. Parque del buen
   Retiro

## SLEEP

1. AC Santo Mauro
2. Aristos
11. Hotel Hesperia
    Madrid
19. Intercontinental
    Castellana Madrid
21. Occidental Miguel
    Angel

0        0.5        1km

# Centro

With Madrid's uninspiring Manzanares river hovering on the western edge of the city, it's left to the wide and equally uninspiring Gran Via to form the city's natural north–south divide. The mercantile boulevard is always packed with traffic and pedestrians; it is Madrid's equivalent to Oxford Street and the retail centre of the city.

The grand early 20th-century buildings are now home to shops, offices and hotels, some of them considerably more aesthetically pleasing than others. The Gran Via was built in three phases over nearly five years, replacing 14 smaller streets, and its construction was viewed as a symbol of Spain moving into the 20th century.

To the south of the Gran Via lies the Puerta del Sol, which marks the epicentre of the city and of Spain. This is the spot from which all distances in Spain are measured. Since it's the nucleus of Madrid's public transport network, it is a popular meeting-place and a focal point for tourists. Unfortunately, the prevalence of visitors inevitably attracts pickpockets, so keep an eye on your possessions.

Although the location is ideal, many of the hotels in this part of town are a little tired, but the recent arrival of Hotel Quo looks set to change all this. Its funky interiors and enthusiastic young staff make this a welcome addition to Madrid's hotel scene.

Mid-priced shops are clustered around Calle de Preciados and Calle Carmen, while some of the larger chain stores line the Gran Via, including the city's largest Zara. There are many little souvenir and dedicated handicraft shops in the area that sell everything from delicious nougat to intricately patterned fans, so it's worth trawling the side streets looking for that authentic Madrid memento.

To the south-east of Sol is the Plaza Santa Ana, a touristy but pleasant square surrounded by cafés and restaurants. Head further east and you'll find the streets of Las Huertas, lined with more places to eat and drink. It's relatively quiet here by day but at night the shuttered doors and windows open to reveal cocktail bars, discos, karaoke joints and music clubs that keep going until the early hours.

Calle Jesus is home to a string of funky little *tapas* bars, such as Los Gatos and Taberna Maceira, where locals and tourists alike work their way along the street enjoying a quick bite to eat and a glass of *tinto* at each one.

The streets here lead down to the Paseo del Prado, where you'll find the city's golden triangle of museums: the Thyssen, the Reina Sofia and, of course, the famous Prado. Madrid's three major museums and galleries are conveniently located within a short walk of each other, although there is far too much to see in just one day.

There are some reasonably priced hotels here, like the Hotel Mora, and perhaps Madrid's most famous hotel, the Ritz. Even if you don't stay here, it's worth dropping by to see the ornate interiors and to enjoy afternoon tea.

0    250    500m

Ⓜ Metro Station

# ■ DRINK

4.   Bar Museo Los Gabrieles
10.  Ducados Café
11.  El Barbu
20.  La Fontana de Oro
27.  Suite
28.  Viva Madrid

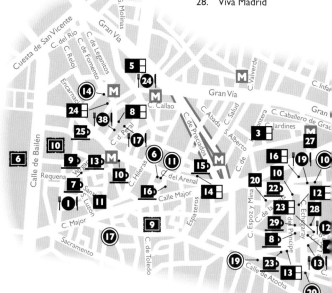

# ☕ SNACK

6.   Café de Circulo de Bellas Artes
7.   Café de los Austrias
9.   Café de Oriente
8.   Café del Espanol
10.  Café del Real
13.  Café Vergara
15.  Casa Labra
16.  Chocolateria San Gines
19.  Los Gatos
22.  Museo del Jamon
23.  Salon del Prado
25.  Taberna del Alabardero
27.  Taberna Maceira
29.  La Trucha

# ■ CULTURE

2.   Centro de Arte Reina Sofi
4.   Museo del Prado
5.   Museo Thyssen Bornemisz
6.   Palacio Real
8.   Plaza de la Cibeles
9.   Plaza Mayor
10.  Plaza Oriente

## EAT

1. Al Norte
3. Balzac
10. Champagneria Gala
12. Cluny
13. La Cueva de Gata
17. Entre Suspiro y Suspiro
19. La Finca de Susana
24. Larios Café
25. Lhardy
38. La Viuda Blanca

## PARTY

6. Joy Madrid
7. Kapital
10. The Room at Stella
11. Palacio Gaviria
13. La Vieja Estacion
14. Café de Chinitas
17. Las Carboneras
19. Café Central
20. Café Jazz Populart

## SHOP

◼ Calle del Carmen
◼ Calle de Preciados

## SLEEP

3. Ateneo Hotel
5. Emperador
8. HH Campomanes
12. Hotel Ingles
13. Hotel Miau
14. Hotel Moderno
16. Hotel Quo
20. Mora
22. The Ritz
23. Suite Prado
24. Tryp Ambassador
27. The Westin Palace
26. Villas Real

# Chueca and Malasana

Just north of the Gran Via lie the districts of Chueca and Malasana, both known for their trendy but laid-back bars, cafés and clubs, all with their own distinctive identities.

Chueca is Madrid's gay quarter, although it's just as popular with the city's trendy non-gay crowd. In fact, many gays now complain that the area is just not gay enough. The focus of the scene is the Plaza de Chueca, which comes alive on summer evenings when all and sundry gather on the terraces of its bars and restaurants. The plaza is undergoing a bit of a revival right now, spurred on by the arrival of Azul Profundo, a concept restaurant owned by top chef Andres Madrigal which offers a unique culinary experience.

The shops here reflect the character of the area – they're bold, colourful, alternative and often outrageous – and range from bargain basements to the exclusive and pricey. Chueca is also a shoe-lovers' heaven, with one street – Calle Augusto Figueroa – devoted almost entirely to footwear.

Fuencarral, which forms the border between Chueca and Malasana, is great for club-wear and low-priced clothes. Towards Recoletos, on the east side of Chueca, you'll find the more up-market fashion shops and

exclusive restaurants and cafés, including Olivera and Indochina, that cater for the business crowd.

Meanwhile, Malasana, stretching west as far as San Bernardo, is more grungy and studenty. It was once the centre of resistance against the French in 1808 and is named after a young seamstress, Manuela Malasana, who was shot by the French invaders for carrying ammunition (her scissors) to the Spanish troops.

In the 1970s it became the focus of the Movida Madrilena, the 'Happening Scene', where bars opened all over the place and drugs were sold on the streets in a time of new-found freedom. In the 1980s the area degenerated into a hang-out for drug users and drunks, but urban renovation has cleaned it up considerably. The main square, Plaza Dos de Mayo, has been redeveloped but the streets to the south of it are still best avoided late at night.

Some streets still look a bit tatty, and that's part of the charm, but the recent arrival of more sophisticated restaurants, such as Nina, looks set to turn Malasana more up-market. However, old favourites such as El Parnasillo and Café del Foro will ensure that Malasana always retains its alternative and slightly eccentric feel.

In this part of the city, pretty much anything goes.

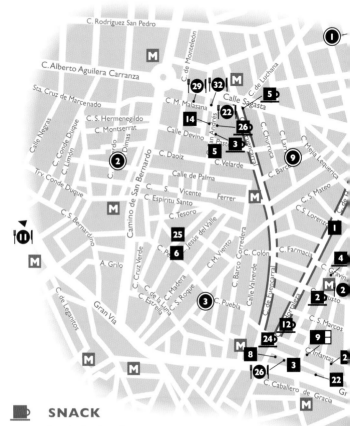

## ☕ SNACK

    2.    La Bardemcilla
    3.    Blue Fish
    4.    Café Acuarela
    5.    Café Commercial
  11.    Café Gijon
  12.    Café Mama Ines
  26.    La Taberna del Foro
  24.    Stop Madrid

 **SLEEP**

    9.    H.R. San Lorenzo
  15.    Hotel Orfila

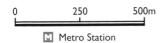

**0      250      500m**

M Metro Station

## DRINK

1. Areia
3. Bar Cock
5. Café del Foro
6. Cafeina
8. Del Diego
13. El Clandestino
14. El Parnasillo
15. El Son
18. EO
24. La Otra Mabana
22. Museo Chicote
23. Olivera
25. Oui
26. Stars Dance Café

## PARTY

1. Barnon
2. Café la Palma
3. El Perro
9. Pacha

## EAT

2. Azul Profundo
8. Café Oliver
11. La Chantarella
20. Indochina
22. La Isla del Tesoro
23. Kikuyu
26. Luna Mulata
29. La Musa
32. Nina

## SHOP

■ Chueca
■ Malasana

# The Old City/La Latina

South of the Gran Via, between the Plaza Mayor, the Palacio Real and San Francisco el Grande, lies the oldest part of Madrid, with the oldest part of all found between the Plaza de la Cebada, Plaza Mayor and the Palacio Real. This is the site of the medieval Muslim town, characterized by winding, often hilly cobbled streets which are now home to exclusive restaurants and wine bars.

Plaza Mayor is the obvious meeting-place, but the area is dotted with other squares that are prettier and less touristy. Head south to the series of squares in La Latina (Plaza de la Paja, Plaza de San Andres, Plaza de la Cebada), which are surrounded by some of the city's coolest and more chilled bars and cafés. Delic, La Musa Latina, Carpanta and Lamiak are hugely popular hang-outs, just far enough away from the centre not to be plagued by tourists. This mainly pedestrianized area is great on a sunny afternoon but comes into its own at night, when crowds of trendy Madrilenos gather here for wine and *tapas*.

One of Madrid's most famous meeting-places, the three-storey El Viajero is a great place to start off the evening, before moving between the different bars. On summer evenings it seems as if there are as

many people on the streets, walking between venues, as there are inside them.

East of here is the colourful working-class neighbourhood of Lavapies, with an ethnic mix of North Africans, Indians, Chinese and Turks. It's home to the city's famous Sunday market, El Rastro, where thousands of people flock in search of bargains, but shops selling cheap clothes and leather are open all week.

To the west of the Plaza Mayor lies Royal Madrid, encompassing the impressive royal palace, the cathedral, the theatre and the Campo del Moro park, beyond which stretches the Casa de Campo wilderness. Tourists and locals sip coffee in atmospheric cafés, such as Café de los Austrias and Café de Oriente, whose beautiful terrace overlooks the palace.

The Old City is naturally the most touristy part of Madrid and some of its restaurants and bars are overpriced, but it's worth paying that little bit extra for the pleasure of the surroundings. This is the prettiest and most atmospheric part of the city; take time off for an afternoon stroll and wonder at the architecture and the history.

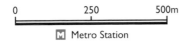

0      250      500m

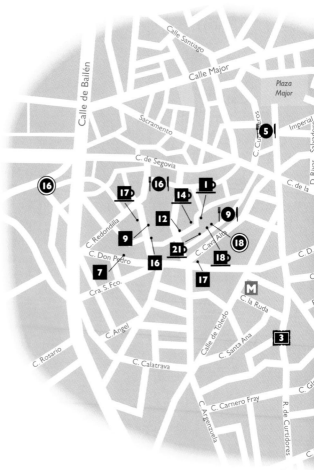

M   Metro Station

Calle Santiago

Calle Major

Plaza Major

Calle de Bailén

Sacramento

C. Cuchilleros

Imperial

C. de la

D. Rivas

Salvadore

C. de Segovia

5

(16)

17

16

14

1

9

C. Redondilla

12

9

21

C. Cava Alta

(18)

C. Don Pedro

16

18

7

17

Cra. S. Fco.

M

C. la Ruda

C.Angel

Calle de Toledo

C. Santa Ana

3

C. Rosario

C. Calatrava

C. Carnero Fray

C. Gl

R. de Curtidores

C. Argenzuela

C.

**PARTY**

15.   Casa Patas
16.   Corral de la Moreria
18.   La Solea

**EAT**

5.   Botin
9.   Casa Lucio
16.   El Estragon Vegetariano

# The Old City/La Latina   local map

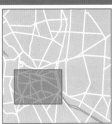

# Salamanca

The swankiest part of Madrid, Salamanca is a grid of wide, elegant avenues lined with designer boutiques, luxury apartments and mansions, galleries and up-market restaurants.

It became the city's rich neighbourhood towards the end of the 19th century when the Marques de Salamanca, a banker, politician and rogue known for his rather dubious business practices, built the first block of houses here, north-east of the city. His own house, on the Paseo de Recoletas, was the first in Madrid to have a flushing lavatory and Salamanca made sure these new developments had the same luxury. Soon other wealthy aristocrats realized the benefits of wider streets and new housing, compared with the narrow, musty streets of old Madrid, and flocked here in droves.

Today Salamanca remains home to Madrid's 'yuppies' and their off-spring (*pijos* or *pijas*) who dress head-to-toe in designer clothes, wear sunglasses year-round, and drive top of the range sports cars.

Many of the city's most exclusive and stylish restaurants are to be found here, including Montana, Matilda and Iroco. Their minimalist, sometimes rather clinical interiors might not be to everyone's taste, but the Salamanca set just can't get enough of them.

You'll also find some of Madrid's most exclusive nightclubs in Salamanca, including Gabana, Moma and Fortuny, where the sports cars parked outside tell you a lot about the type of people inside.

While central Madrid is compact and manageable by foot, here in Salamanca the wide, long avenues mean you'll have to drive, or rely more on taxis to get from one venue to the next.

The roads can get quite busy and on the main shopping streets the pavements become thick with people, particularly between 6pm and the time most shops close, between 8 and 9pm.

Apart from its restaurants and clubs, the main reason to come to Salamanca is for its shopping. Top designer stores are mainly found on calles Jorge Juan, Ortega y Gasset, Serrano and Juan Bravo, while there are cheaper stores towards the east end of Calle Goya and on Calle Alcala. Private art galleries line Calle Claudio Coello, which, along with Serrano and Lagasca, is one of the oldest streets in Salamanca. They are narrower and the shops are smaller and closer together, making it a good area for browsing and window shopping.

To the far east of Salamanca is Madrid's famous bullfighting arena, Las Ventas, while to the west is its grand avenue, the Paseo de la Castellana. Many of the city's largest and luxurious business hotels – the Hotel Hesperia Madrid, Hotel Villa Magna and the Gran Meliá Fénix – are located along this wide thoroughfare, amid the plush office blocks of leading banks and insurance companies.

South of Salamanca is the beautiful Parque del Retiro, where Madrilenos like to take a leisurely stroll all year round.

C. Diego de León

Calle de Maldonado

Calle de Juan Bravo

Calle de Padilla

C. de José Ortega y Gasset

C. de Don Ramón de la Cruz

C. de Ayala

C. de Hermosilla

Calle de Goya

C. de Jorge Juan

C. de Villanueva

C. del Conde Aranda

Calle de Alcalá

Calle de O'Donnell

C. Duque

C. Diego de L

C. de Maldon

Calle de Padil

Pl.
Marqués
de Salamanca

Paseo de la Castellana

Calle de Serrano

Calle de Claudio Coello

Calle de Núñez de Balboa

Calle de Castelló

Calle de Príncipe de Vergara

C. del General Pardiñas

C. de Príncipe de Vergara

Calle de Serrano

C. de ...pleros

Av. Méjico

0      250      500m

M Metro Station

## DRINK

2. Balmoral
21. Geografic Club

## PARTY

5. Gabana 1800

Calle de Juan Bravo

Calle de Francisco Silvela

C. de Alcántara

C. de Cartagena

C. de José Ortega y Gasset

C. de Don Ramón de la Cruz

de Peñalver

Calle de Alcalá

Calle de Goya

. de Jorge Juan

## SNACK

20. Jose Luiz
28. La Timba

## SLEEP

4. Bauza
6. Gran Hotel Velazquez
7. Gran Meliá Fénix
10. Hotel Adler
17. Hotel Wellington
18. Husa Serrano Royal
25. Villa Magna

## EAT

4. Bauza
6. Brasserie de Lista
14. Le Dragon
18. Entretapas y Vinos
21. Iroco
26. Matilda
27. Montana
28. Mumbai Massala
30. Nicolas
31. Nilo
33. Reche
36. Teatriz
37. Thai Gardens

## SHOP

Calle de Jorge Juan 14 y 14 Bis
Calle de José Ortega y Gasset
Calle de Serrano

# sleep...

Although Madrid boasts some exceptionally stylish and luxurious hotels, in general the standard and variety of its accommodation falls behind that of other major cities. While the design/boutique hotel phenomenon has already swept across the rest of Europe, it has only just started to make an impact in Madrid. However, those that have opened here, including HH Campomanes, Bauza and Hotel Quo, are quickly making their mark and their success is likely to spur the arrival of more hotels styled in a similar manner. Even some of the more traditional establishments are adopting a more modern, minimalist look when they undergo refurbishment in an attempt to appeal to a new generation of traveller.

As Madrid is so compact, the location of your hotel is not as important as it might be in larger cities. However, if you are a light sleeper, avoid hotels around Puerta del Sol and the Gran Via where it can get rather noisy, especially at weekends.

Madrid's most elegant hotels, such as the Santo Mauro and the Orfila, are tucked away in quiet, leafy streets in the Chamberi area or, like the Hotel Adler and Hotel Wellington, are to be found in the Salamanca district. Even these are only a short metro or taxi ride away from the heart of the city.

Along the Paseo de la Castellana you'll find the international chain hotels, such as the InterContinental and the Villa Magna, a Park Hyatt, which cater for a corporate crowd during the week but offer some great-value deals for weekend guests.

Although Madrid's hotel industry is not as advanced as in London or Paris, investment has been made in recent years to improve overall standards. A tightening of laws on a range of issues including hygiene and bathrooms-per-person have led to some much-needed improvements in the budget sector. If you're booking budget accommodation and want a bath instead of a shower, mention this when you make your reservation.

The best deals are to be had in August, when room prices can fall by up to 50%, but be aware that at this time temperatures can be uncomfortably high and many restaurants, shops and bars close.

Prices quoted here are per room per night, ranging from a standard double room in the low season to a suite in high season.

These hotels have been rated according to their style, location and atmosphere. 'Style' takes into account the furnishings and the appearance of the hotel inside and out. 'Atmosphere' considers the feel of the place: it might be super-stylish but nevertheless as inviting as a dentist's waiting room; again, it might be decorated like your granny's sitting room but still manage to generate a great ambience. 'Location' assesses how central and convenient the hotels are for shops, restaurants and tourist attractions.

**Our top ten hotels in Madrid are:**
1. AC Santo Mauro
2. Hotel Adler
3. Hotel Orfila
4. The Ritz
5. Hotel Quo
6. Hotel Hesperia Madrid
7. Bauza Hotel
8. Villa Magna
9. Villa Real
10. Hotel Wellington

**Our top five hotels for style are:**
1. AC Santo Mauro
2. Bauza Hotel
3. Hotel Adler
4. Hotel Orfila
5. The Ritz

**Our top five hotels for atmosphere are:**
1. AC Santo Mauro
2. Hotel Adler
3. Hotel Orfila
4. Hotel Quo
5. The Ritz

**Our top five hotels for location are:**
1. Hotel Quo
2. The Ritz
3. HH Campomanes
4. Hotel Orfila
5. Villa Real

### AC Santo Mauro, Zurbano 36, Chamberi.
Tel: 91 319 6900 www.ac-hotels.com
Rates: €318–909

This beautiful, elegant hotel is where the Beckhams stayed while they were searching for a permanent Madrid address. Need we say more? It's the former residence of the Marquis of Santo Mauro and is located in a quiet, leafy street in the wealthy Chamberi district where the Spanish nobility once lived. There are only 51 bedrooms, which is surprising considering the vastness of the lobby and public areas. The small number of guests makes the hotel particularly intimate and exclusive, which no doubt appealed to David and Victoria. There's a fabulous garden and terrace restaurant, a grand library and an indoor pool. Rooms are modern, sleek and super-luxurious and have all that you'd expect from a top five-star hotel. The staff are charming and discreet, as is demanded.

Style 10, Atmosphere 10, Location 9

### Aristos, Avenida de Pio XII.
Tel: 91 345 0450
Rates: €120–163

Considering that this hotel is home to one of Madrid's most revered restaurants, it's a pretty low-key affair. Certainly nothing to look at from the outside, this three-star hotel doesn't seem to be worthy of housing the super-stylish El Chaflan restaurant (see page 71). It's on a busy road in a nondescript, residential area north of the city, about a 10-minute metro ride from the city centre. It aspires to be a design hotel but doesn't quite manage it. Its rooms, however, are stylish enough, with an unusual cream and cherry red colour scheme. There's no breakfast room but room service is available. The real bonus is that room-service lunch, dinner and snacks can also be ordered from El Chaflan. Guests get preferential treatment when it comes to booking a table at the restaurant, however, so it's worth staying here if you're a dedicated foodie.

**Style 8, Atmosphere 8, Location 5**

**Ateneo Hotel, Calle Montera 22, Centro.**
Tel: 91 521 2912 www.ateneohotel.com
Rates: €100–130

Calle Montera is the focal point of Madrid's downtown red-light district, so if you don't want to have to wend your way past scantily clad prostitutes and their shifty-looking clients, this hotel is best avoided. However, in this open-minded city, the seedy goings-on in this part of town simply don't perturb the locals, so why let them bother you? This three-star hotel is simple, modern and smart, with the benefit of a super-central location (equidistant from the Prado Museum, the Royal Palace and the Reina Sofia Museum of Modern Art) without the expense. It has 38 rooms and suites, all with striking red-and-gold-striped bed-covers and large wooden headboards. Some are loft-style rooms with skylights, and three spacious rooms are specifically designed for families.

**Style 7, Atmosphere 7, Location 7**

**Bauza Hotel, Calle Goya 79, Salamanca.**
Tel: 91 435 7545 www.hotelbauza.com
Rates: €126–248

One of the few design hotels in Madrid, this sleek, highly fashion-able hotel has all the right ingredients – a funky restaurant (see page 61), a cool, minimalist lobby, a gym, sauna and beautiful staff. It has 177 rooms and suites and seven long-stay apart-ments, some with large, decked terraces but all decorated in understated, neutral tones. Rooms also have pay and satellite TV, films and video games, and spacious bathrooms. They're just made for chilling out, but if you prefer to mingle with other guests, you can relax in the café or curl up with a book in front of the fireplace in the library. The hotel is located in the busy Goya shopping district in Salamanca, 2 minutes from the Cortes Ingles department store and just a 10-minute stroll from the

Retiro Park. The Goya metro, a stone's throw away, will take you into the city centre in a matter of minutes.

**Style 9, Atmosphere 8, Location 8**

**Emperador, Gran Via 53, Centro.**
Tel: 91 547 2817 www.emperadorhotel.com
Rates: €209–305

This hotel's best feature is its rooftop pool, although it's only open from mid-June to mid-September (non-residents are invited to use it for a fee). From here, you'll also get stunning views across the city. Apart from that, this four-star hotel is rather bland. All of its 232 rooms are individually decorated, some of

them with a rather garish mix of colours and patterns. Although it's on the busy Gran Via, rooms are surprisingly quiet. There is a small gym and a hairdresser private members' club, open to guests, which tends to get filled with smoke and business people. The restaurant serves breakfast and lunch, but is only worth checking out at breakfast-time.

**Style 6, Atmosphere 7, Location 7**

**Gran Hotel Velázquez, Velázquez 62, Salamanca.**
Tel: 91 575 2800 www.chh.es
Rates: € 125–375

Another of the old-style hotels in the Salamanca district, the four-star Gran Hotel Velázquez has light and cheery bedrooms with quaint pastel blue and white flowery bed-covers and matching curtains. There are 144 rooms in all, including 75 suites that are super-spacious. The overall feel is rather formal and conservative during the week when the majority of guests are here for a conference or a meeting. However, the hotel takes on a more relaxed feel at weekends and has all the extras you'll need for a leisure break. There's even a gift shop and a hair salon. The bar, a popular meeting-place for the Salamanca crowd, has enough seating for everyone. The hotel's website has handy virtual tours of each room type so you can choose one to suit you.

**Style 8, Atmosphere 7, Location 9**

### Gran Meliá Fénix, Hermosilla 2, Salamanca.
Tel: 91 431 6700 www.solmelia.com
Rates: €300–515

Scarlet velvet *chaises*, ornate rugs, embroidered bedding and exquisite art all add to the elegant and refined feel of this hotel. The 225-room Gran Meliá Fénix occupies a national heritage building that dates back to the early 1950s but was completely refurbished in 2002. It sits just off the Plaza Colon, in the prestigious Salamanca district. Its grand, circular lobby has a stunning stained-glass atrium and enormous flower arrangements, and is a perfect setting for the pianist, who performs every day. Staff are the mature, well-experienced variety and the door staff are particularly cheerful. In the week, guests are mostly here on business so the atmosphere is rather stuffy and formal, but at weekends the tourist arrivals lighten the mood. Maybe it's because they know they're only paying half as much as their corporate counterparts?

**Style 8, Atmosphere 8, Location 9**

### HH Campomanes, Calle Campomanes 4, Centro.
Tel: 91 548 8548 www.hhcampomanes.com
Rates: €84–144

One of the more recent additions to Madrid's hotel scene, this establishment is another of the new breed of design hotels.

Opened in 2001, it is ideally located for the Teatro Real, Metro Opera and all the restaurants and bars in this part of the city. However, it's tucked away on a smart, quiet street so you won't suffer any of the disturbances of being in the thick of things, although it's also just two doors away from one of Madrid's funkiest restaurants, La Viuda Blanca (see page 93). There is a tiny but cosy lobby and a café where breakfast is served (self-service continental breakfast is included in the room rate). The 30 bed-rooms, two of them mini-suites, are tastefully decorated in beiges and charcoal greys. White walls and minimalism are the name of the game.

**Style 9, Atmosphere 8, Location 9**

**Hostal H.R. San Lorenzo, Calle Clavel 8, Chueca.**
Tel: 91 521 3057 www.hotel-sanlorenzo.com
Rates: €75–80

Just off the Gran Via, in the fashionable Chueca area, this hostel has only recently been upgraded to three-star hotel standard. It is, however, one of the better three-star options in the city and, coupled with its central location, is a good choice if you want to skimp on hotel costs and have more spending money. Its rooms are simple but pretty, with blue and white bed-covers and flow-ery curtains, all kept spotlessly clean. Some have balconies with flower boxes. Despite the low price, you'll still get a private safe,

direct-dial telephone and a hairdryer. The first-floor lobby
lounge and café are pleasant enough for hanging out, but there
are some more interesting cafés and restaurants right on your
doorstep.

**Style 6, Atmosphere 6, Location 7**

**Hotel Adler, Velázquez 33, Salamanca.**
Tel: 91 426 3220 www.iova-sa.com
Rates: €270–450

An absolute gem of a hotel right in the heart of the swanky
Salamanca district, the Hotel Adler is simply surrounded by
designer shops and only a 2-minute walk away from the Retiro
Park. It's located on the corner of Velázquez and Goya, two of

Madrid's most distinguished streets. This recently opened hotel was designed by Pascua Ortega, who has chosen a smart, classic but contemporary look infused with the homeliness of an English country house. It is equipped with the most up-to-date technology, but has retained the grandeur of its 19th-century building. Its 45 deluxe rooms are classic but modern in style, painted in neutral tones mixed with a splash of colour and tartan. The restaurant serves *haute cuisine* and there's a small, cosy bar. Privately owned, this five-star hotel has a warm, personal feel and soon staff will be greeting you by name.

**Style 9, Atmosphere 10, Location 9**

**Hotel Hesperia Madrid, Paseo de la Castellana 57, Salamanca.**
Tel: 91 210 8800 www.hoteles-hesperia.es
Rates: €357–743

Billed as Madrid's first five-star contemporary hotel and a member of the exclusive 'Leading Hotels of the World' collection, this hotel set new standards in accommodation in the capital when it opened in 2000. It is located in the financial and diplomatic area and is, on weekdays, mainly a business hotel. Its public areas were designed by Pascua Ortega, known for his work in the Teatro Real and the Hotel Adler. The overall look is Oriental chic (*feng*

*shui* meets cutting-edge design). The 139 rooms and 32 suites are light and spacious, and have all the latest mod-cons and luxuries, including Bulgari delicacies in the bathroom. The hotel is home to Santceloni (see page 89), one of Madrid's top restaurants, and an intimate Scotch bar serving over 70 single-malt whiskies. Although there are only limited health facilities, guests get free access to the nearby Metropolitan, one of the city's most prestigious health clubs.

**Style 9, Atmosphere 8, Location 8**

**Hotel Ingles, Calle Echegaray 8, Centro.**
Tel: 91 429 6551
Rates: €75–112

This traditional three-star hotel is clean and compact and has a great central location. However, it is surrounded by the bars and

nightclubs on Echegaray so it's not for someone looking to escape the crowds. Avoid rooms overlooking the street since they can be noisy, particularly at the weekends. The hotel is family-run and only has 58 rooms, so it has an intimate, personal feel. Its public rooms are cheery and sunny and, considering the hotel dates back 150 years, its decoration has been very well maintained. The buffet breakfast is excellent value at only €5. Facilities are good for a three-star hotel and include a small but well-equipped fitness centre, a cocktail bar, coffee shop, a gift shop and private parking.

**Style 6, Atmosphere 8, Location 8**

**Hotel Miau, Calle Principe 26, Centro.**
Tel: 91 369 7120
Rates: €60–95

With such a prime position, on the corner of Plaza de Santa Ana, right in the heart of downtown Madrid and a stone's throw from some of its best bars and restaurants, it's no wonder this little gem of a hotel decided to double in size this year. It now has 40 rooms, with around half of them having tiny balconies which overlook the Plaza de Santa Ana. Rooms are simple and light, with white walls, shuttered white windows, mint-green bedding, and a large contemporary painting above each bed. Each room has a television with international channels, a small, spotlessly clean bathroom with a shower and good air-conditioning. There's a café and restaurant of the same name next door with a popular terrace in the summer. Request a room with a view when you book, or risk getting one of the few rooms that overlook a tiny, shabby courtyard where the laundry is done.

**Style 8, Atmosphere 7, Location 9**

**Hotel Moderno, Calle Arenal 2, Centro.**
Tel: 91 531 9900/532 1792 www.hotel-moderno.com
Rates: €85–150

Don't be fooled by the name – this hotel is certainly not modern.
In fact, with their dark wood headboards, sludgy green-brown
colour schemes and chintzy flowery curtains, its rooms are rather

dated (although the bathrooms and corridors are more tastefully
decorated). However, this hotel wins points for its central location
(just off the Puerta del Sol) and for the fact that 25 of the 97
rooms have their own private terraces. Admittedly, the balconies
are furnished with cheap-looking fake grass and plastic tables and
chairs, but since any kind of terrace is a rarity in Madrid, it's a treat
to have somewhere pleasant to sit and unwind at the end of a hard
day's sightseeing. The hotel also has a pleasant lounge area, a bright,
sunny breakfast room and, of course, a good central
location. This area can be noisy at night but all the rooms are dou-
ble-glazed.

Style 6, Atmosphere 7, Location 8

**Hotel Orfila, Orfila 6, Chamberi.**
Tel: 91 702 7700 www.hotelorfila.com
Rates: €296–1,128

A beautiful hotel that exudes charm and prestige, the Hotel
Orfila is a member of the exclusive Relais & Chateaux group so
you can rest assured the service will be top-notch too. This
19th-century palace, in a leafy residential street in the Chamberi

district, was converted to a hotel in the 1990s but still has that
palace feel. Its lobby, with its huge floral displays and *chaises
longues*, has welcomed many dignitaries and VIPs, but the highly
professional staff treat all guests with equal reverence. With only
28 rooms and four suites, the service is particularly personal.
Each room is different but all are exquisitely decorated. Those
with attic-style sloping ceilings have the most character. All
rooms have hydro-massage baths and the usual array of high-
tech gadgets, but they're discreetly tucked away so they don't
interfere with the traditional design. All guests are welcomed
with a bottle of *cava*.

Style 9, Atmosphere 10, Location 9

**Hotel Quo, Sevilla 4, Centro.**
Tel: 91 532 9049 www.hotelesquo.com
Rates: €172–200

One of the latest arrivals on Madrid's hotel scene, this hotel is
geared towards young, discerning travellers who appreciate style
and design but want a chilled-out, informal atmosphere. The

hotel is located in the Puerta del Sol, right in the heart of the city, where until now there has been a distinct lack of stylish

options. The corner building, originally 19th-century, has undergone a complete transformation inside, replete with funky, designer furniture. The overall look is contemporary but homely, especially the comfortable sofas and armchairs in the lobby. There are 61 bedrooms, six with balconies and one junior suite. All have a black and white colour scheme, with incredibly large beds. Pillows are also larger than the norm, and there's a 'pillow menu' if you want one that's harder or softer. The hotel's restaurant also follows the funky black and white theme, and it's open for breakfast, lunch and dinner. Food is contemporary international and tables are laid out in rows, so odds-on you'll be socializing with the other style-savvy guests.

**Style 9, Atmosphere 9, Location 9**

**Hotel Wellington, Velázquez 8, Salamanca.**
Tel: 91 575 4400 www.hotel-wellington.com
Rates: €240–400

One of only a handful of hotels in the city with a swimming pool, this traditional hotel is a good choice in the height of the summer. Its rooftop outdoor pool is open from mid-June to mid-

September and has a large sun terrace. The five-star hotel was opened in 1952 and its marble floors, chandeliers and lobby frescos have been maintained in good order. It was once one of Madrid's finest hotels but others have come a long way since and upped the competition. Rooms here have recently been refurbished and are rather masculine in style, with striped bed-covers. Perhaps this is to cater for the macho bullfighters who stay here during the bullfighting season. The hotel also has a cosy English

bar, a coffee shop, an à la carte restaurant (the Goizeko Wellington), a sauna and a hairdresser. It is ideally located in the Salamanca district, just a short walk away from the Retiro Park, and surrounded by some of Madrid's finest shops.

**Style 8, Atmosphere 8, Location 9**

**Husa Serrano Royal, Marques de Villamejor 8, Salamanca.**
Tel: 91 576 9626 www.husa.es
Rates: €141–191

If you want an exclusive location without paying a hefty price for it, try this small four-star hotel. In a quiet little street between the grand Paseo de la Castellana and Serrano, the city's answer to Bond Street, this 34-room hotel has recently been renovated. Its bedrooms are painted in soothing creams and pastels and are ideal for relaxation after a day of retail therapy. After a bath, wrap yourself in one of the thick, comfy bathroom towels and settle down to catch up with the news on satellite TV before venturing out to one of Salamanca's top restaurants. Staff are polite and friendly and there's a delicious buffet breakfast laid out in a delightful little breakfast room.

**Style 7, Atmosphere 8, Location 9**

### InterContinental Castellana Madrid, Paseo de la Castellana 49, Chamberi.
Tel: 91 700 7300 www.madrid.intercontinental.com
Rates: €365–4,500

Primarily for business travellers, this huge 307-room hotel lends itself well to leisure stays at the weekends when rates fall dramatically. It's a popular meeting-place and its huge, high-ceilinged lobby is always bustling with people. If you prefer the kind of hotel where you can remain anonymous and come and go without even being noticed, this is for you. That doesn't mean that you won't get good, personal service if you want it. Although the hotel is part of an international chain, it still has lots of character and charm. Some of its bedrooms are a bit chintzy, but they do have all the necessary facilities. Pay a bit extra and you can upgrade to a club room where you'll have access to an exclusive club lounge. Other special features include an outdoor garden and a decent, 24-hour health club.

Style 8, Atmosphere 8, Location 8

**Mora, Paseo del Prado 32, Centro.**
Tel: 91 420 0564
Rates: €63–69

Although its facilities only win this hotel two stars, it deserves more in terms of its service, location and its fresh, bright interior. It's in an attractive historic building right opposite the Prado, making it ideal for a cultural break. The hotel was refurbished in

2001 and although it won't pick up any style awards, it's pleasant enough. Its lobby is as grand as you're likely to see in a two-star hotel, with marble pillars, chandeliers and a polished marble floor. The 62 rooms lack character but they are clean and light. Some only have showers and are slightly cheaper.

Style 7, Atmosphere 7, Location 8

### Occidental Miguel Angel, Calle Miguel Angel 299, Chamberi.
Tel: 91 442 0022 www.occidentalmiguelangel.com
Rates: €155–395

This hotel is home to La Broche, one of Madrid's top restaurants, but it couldn't be more different from its fashionably stark and minimalist restaurant. Like Hotel Aristos, where you'll find El Chaflan restaurant, the Miguel Angel is disappointingly mediocre when compared with La Broche. Its interiors are old-fashioned and uninspiring, but its 263 bedrooms have everything you'd

expect. The staff here are particularly on the ball, and are well trained to deal with the most demanding of corporate guests. The hotel is located just off the Paseo de la Castellana, in the heart of Madrid's financial district, so its bar is a popular meeting-place for local business people. Another redeeming feature is its terrace garden, which is a pleasant spot for a romantic drink.

**Style 5, Atmosphere 6, Location 8**

● **The Ritz, Plaza de la Lealtad 5, Centro.**
Tel: 91 701 6767 www.ritzmadrid.com
Rates: €357–1,016

Perhaps Madrid's most famous hotel, and one of the original
grand hotels of Europe, the Hotel Ritz was built on the orders
of King Alfonso XIII who wanted a hotel to rival the Ritz in
Paris. It opened in 1910 with much royal fanfare and is a fine

example of a Belle Epoque building. Staff make you feel as if
you're privileged to be here, but then maybe that's to be expected with a guest list of such high calibre – they are more used to
dealing with the likes of George Bush, Tony Blair, Madonna, Brad
Pitt and, er… the Spice Girls. Pretty much every head of state
and A-list celebrity has passed through the hotel's swing doors.
Its 137 rooms overlook the hotel's gardens, the Lealtad Square
or the Prado; all have hand-made carpets, embroidered linens
and original antiques as well as all the necessary mod-cons. Its
lobby lounge is hugely popular for Sunday brunch and afternoon
tea, and its terrace and gardens are a pleasant spot for some
lunch or *tapas*. If you splash out on a suite, you'll get a free private airport transfer.

**Style 9, Atmosphere 9, Location 9**

**Suite Prado, Calle Manuel Fernandez y Gonzalez 10, Centro.**
Tel: 91 420 2318 www.suiteprado.com
Rates: €153–172

For the flexibility of self-catering, this hotel is the perfect option. It consists entirely of suites, all of which have separate dining

rooms and kitchens, so you can cook your own breakfast or prepare lunch. However, with Madrid's splendid selection of restaurants and cafés, and many of them just a short walk away, it would be a shame to spend too much time in the kitchen. Suites are simply and tastefully decorated in warm, pastel colours and bathrooms are generously sized with wall-to-wall marble. Some rooms are large enough to accommodate three people. If you stay here and choose to join the crowds at Viva Madrid, one of the city's most lively bars, you only have to stumble along a few steps and you'll be back home.

**Style 7, Atmosphere 7, Location 8**

**Tryp Ambassador, Cuesta de Santo Domingo 5/7, Centro.**
Tel: 91 541 6700 www.solmelia.com
Rates: €259–554.

In the old palace of the Duques de Granada de Ega, the four-star Tryp Ambassador has more character than the other Tryp hotels in Madrid. It has retained much of its original structure and has been refurbished in the old, lavish style, with elegant furniture, antiques and palms. There are 182 rooms, including 24 suites, all with interactive satellite TV. Some of them are a little bit chintzy in style, but all the essential amenities are there. The hotel's main

restaurant, El Invernadero, serves traditional Spanish food while its less formal Bar Entrepatios is good for sandwiches, *tapas* and cakes. The highlight, however, is the delightful, covered winter garden, decorated with lights. The hotel is ideally located, just south of the Gran Via and close to the Royal Palace, but on a quiet road away from the hustle and bustle of this touristy part of the city.

**Style 7, Atmosphere 7, Location 9**

**Villa Magna, Paseo de la Castellana 22, Salamanca.**
Tel: 91 587 1234 www.madrid.hyatt.com
Rates: €321–815

Now part of the Hyatt chain, according to some this hotel has lost some of its former charm. However, you only have to spend 5 minutes in its glitzy lobby to see that it still manages to attract plenty of well-heeled tourists and expense-account businesspeople. It's situated in pretty gardens and backs on to Madrid's most up-market shopping street, Serrano. In fact, from the hotel you can get direct access into the Serrano Cortes Ingles department store. The service is top-notch – its corporate guests wouldn't be content with anything less – and the concierge is extremely helpful. There are two highly regarded restaurants, the fine Chinese restaurant, Tse Yang, and the equally swanky

Mediterranean restaurant, Le Divellec. The hotel's 182 rooms are luxuriously decorated in rich, earthy tones and have all the usual amenities. Its Club Olympus Fitness Centre has a sauna, steam bath, relaxation room and a multi-station gym with the latest cardiovascular equipment.

**Style 8, Atmosphere 8, Location 9**

**Villa Real, Plaza de las Cortes 10, Centro.**
Tel: 91 420 3767 www.derbyhotels.es
Rates: €140–500

All the rooms have impressive views at this elegant, five-star hotel, located just a 2-minute walk from the Prado and Retiro Park. Its 115 rooms and suites are particularly luxurious, and parquet floors, root mahogany furniture and tan leather sofas make them stylish without being too modern. Many are split level, with the bed on a raised platform to separate it from the sitting area, and some have balconies large enough to sit on. There are also 19 spacious duplex suites. Bedrooms and public areas are decorated with valuable art, sculptures and antiques,

adding to the overall feeling of grandeur. The Villa Real is part of the Derby Hotels chain, owned by Catalan archaeologist Jordi Clos, who has chosen to display his private Roman mosaic collection around the hotel. There are two restaurants, the Europa (Mediterranean) and East 47 (contemporary), as well as a sauna, gym, café and bar. Dogs are allowed.

**Style 8, Atmosphere 8, Location 9**

**The Westin Palace, Plaza de las Cortes 7, Centro.**
Tel: 91 360 8000 www.westin.com/palacemadrid
Rates: €439–879

Originally a palace commissioned by King Alfonso XIII in 1912, this hotel is a landmark in Madrid. Its beautifully ornate lobby, with spectacular coloured glass atrium, is worth checking out even if you don't end up staying here. The hotel has been renovated but has kept its palatial splendour. Its most recent addition is an ultra-modern fitness centre where you can also go for a sauna, massage or solarium. There are 465 rooms and suites, all with Westin's super-comfortable trademark 'Heavenly Bed'. The bar is an elegant spot for a coffee or cocktail, and with Spain's parliament buildings just across the road, you might find yourself standing next to a politician or two. The hotel is on the Plaza de las Cortes, right in the middle of Madrid's so-called Golden Triangle of Art – the Prado, the Thyssen and the Reina Sofia.

**Style 8, Atmosphere 8, Location 9**

# Updates and notes...

# eat...

Fried egg and chips to start, meat and offal stew, tripe or suckling pig for the main course, and rice pudding to finish? Hmmm, maybe not.

Madrid's hearty peasant food might not be to everyone's taste, but luckily these days the city's restaurant scene has matured and diversified to become as cosmopolitan and sophisticated as you'll find anywhere in the world's major cities.

An influx of creative and innovative chefs from different regions of Spain, and from further afield, has given rise to a wealth of up-market, contemporary restaurants that would easily stand their ground against the best of London, Paris or New York.

Santceloni, El Chaflan and La Broche are three such restaurants, and all have rightly earned a name for themselves on the international scene. Prices are high by Madrid standards but are still great value when you compare them to similar restaurants in other European cities. Furthermore, you won't have to book months ahead to secure a table.

In Salamanca there are dozens of fabulous, high-class restaurants, all sporting that cool, minimalist look that appeals to today's discerning diner. The likes of Matilda, Montana, Iroco and Nilo, to name but a few, all cater for the well-heeled Salamanca crowd which likes to be seen in the right places and which appreciates creative, exquisitely presented and fashionable (usually fusion) food.

Salamanca is also home to Le Dragon (Chinese), Mumbai Masala (Indian) and Thai Gardens (you've guessed it), all fine examples in their particular field and nothing like your local back home. As recently as the mid-1990s there were few international restaurants in Madrid, but now you will find everything from great Mexican (Entre Suspiro Y Suspiro) to Japanese (Tao).

Vegetarian food is also something that has only recently caught on here, but now El Estragon Vegetariano and La Isla del Tesoro, among others, have changed all that. Sunday brunch is also starting to permeate Madrid's dining habits, thanks to such forward-thinking establishments as Café Oliver and Nina.

But no visit to Madrid would be complete without sampling some local fare, and Casa Lucio is the place to do it. Politicians and VIPs have been enjoying its simple, well-prepared food for decades.

Wherever you eat, don't go too early. Madrilenos rarely eat lunch before 2pm and tend to arrive for dinner at around 10pm, and even later in the summer. Most restaurants don't open until 9pm and if you're already there at that time, you're obviously a tourist. The dining experience is usually a long, leisurely one, even at lunchtime, so allow plenty of time. If you prefer a quicker, lighter bite to eat, try one of Madrid's *tapas* bars (see Snack). Most restaurants offer a great-value set menu (*menu del dia*) at lunchtimes, including the most up-market ones, so you can sample the city's top cuisine even if you're on a tight budget.

Reservations are advised for all of the restaurants listed below (unless otherwise stated), especially at the weekends, and although there is no set rule for tipping, it's usual to leave 10%.

All the restaurants in this section are rated in terms of food, service and atmosphere. The price given is based on the cost of a three-course meal for one with half a bottle of wine.

**Our top ten restaurants in Madrid are:**
1. Santceloni
2. El Chaflan
3. Matilda
4. Montana
5. La Viuda Blanca
6. La Chantarella
7. La Broche
8. Balzac
9. Botin
10. Casa Lucio

**Our top five restaurants for food are:**
1. Santceloni
2. El Chaflan
3. La Chantarella
4. Montana
5. Nicolas

**Our top five restaurants for service are:**
1. Montana
2. Thai Gardens
3. Santceloni
4. Casa Lucio
5. El Chaflan

**Our top five restaurants for atmosphere are:**
1. La Viuda Blanca
2. Matilda
3. Nilo
4. Balzac
5. Botin

### Al Norte, San Nicolás 8, Centro.
Tel: 91 547 2222
Open: 2–4pm, 9pm–midnight daily
€35

Set just behind the Palacio Real in an unassuming modern build-ing, hidden in a narrow side street, Al Norte is a very chic affair. Sedate businessmen and well-heeled locals sink into the deep red velvet-covered banquettes to enjoy the Northern Spanish cuisine. Classic one-time peasant dishes are dressed up with sophisticated ingredients and a modern take. The menu, which changes monthly, makes the most of a traditional Spanish larder; however, it sometimes falls slightly short of the mark. The wait-ers glide around effortlessly, advising on the choice of fine wines and tempting dishes. Intended as a comfortable and fashionable retreat for the affluent locals, it won't win any design awards but does enough to make you feel very grown-up. The food, the service and the stylish modern décor are the embodiment of simplicity and elegance.

Food 7/8, Service 8, Atmosphere 7/8

### Azul Profundo, Plaza de Chueca 4, Chueca.
Tel: 91 532 2564
Open: 1.30–3.30pm, 9–11.30pm.
Closed Sunday night and Monday.
€37

Run by Andres Madrigal, of Balzac fame, this relative newcomer offers a dining experience like no other. There's an 11-course set menu for lunch and dinner, and there's absolutely no choice, so you're in for the long haul. The selection of dishes changes every

eight to 10 days, depending on the season and, presumably, the mood of the chef. Don't be daunted by the thought of 11 courses, though. They come in minuscule portions, served sometimes in tiny glasses or ceramic spoons. Most are a complex mix of flavours and textures, some more pleasing than others, but all are a work of art. Staff describe each dish as it is served, explaining the contents and how best to devour them. Whether or not you enjoy the whole process, which leaves little time for relaxation and chat, it's certainly a novelty. This tiny, cool-looking restaurant, with its strong blue colour scheme inside and out, stands out in the otherwise rather tatty Plaza de Chueca and has quickly attracted the alternative Chueca crowd, which is always looking for something different.

**Food 9, Service 8, Atmosphere 7**

**Balzac, Calle de Moreto 7, Salamanca.**
Tel: 91 420 0613
Open: 1.30–4pm, 9pm–12.30am.
Closed Saturday lunch and Sunday.                    €40

This elegant restaurant, in a rather grand street on the edge of the Retiro Park, is home to one of Madrid's rising young culinary stars. Chef Andres Madrigal has become one of the leading figures in the shake-up of the city's restaurant scene (see also Azul

Profundo, page 59), with his fusion of modern Spanish cooking and flavours of Provence. Some of the dishes are particularly 'out there', like the *wasabi* ice cream, but most are more traditionally based with a strong emphasis on fish, wild game and seasonal vegetables. The *menu degustacion* is a very reasonable €58 per person. The restaurant itself is spread across a number of separate dining rooms, all furnished with elegant leather dining chairs and white linen tablecloths. Its lemon and apricot walls give it a warmth that most of its minimalist counterparts lack, while pieces of modern art add a splash of extra colour.

**Food 9, Service 8, Atmosphere 9**

**Bauza, Calle Goya 79, Salamanca.**
Tel: 91 435 7545
Open: 1.30–4pm, 8.30–11.30pm daily                          €30

On the first floor of the trendy Bauza Hotel, away from the manic shoppers on Calle Goya, this restaurant has all that you'd expect from a design hotel. Plenty of glass, tones of white and beige and Zen-like minimalism make this the epitome of the contemporary dining experience. The only dash of colour is supplied by huge flowers on each table – that is, until the food arrives. The Mediterranean cuisine (with the ubiquitous Asian touch) is served up looking as stylish as the surroundings, and in fashionably small portions. This is a good place to come if you're on your own, since you can entertain yourself by watching the Salamanca set out spending their money in the street below. If you arrive a little early, perch at the bar and enjoy a well-made cocktail or eye up your new neighbours. The only thing that might disappoint is the service, but then isn't that something else you've come to expect from the designer experience?!

**Food 8, Service 6, Atmosphere 7**

**Botin, Calle Cuchilleros 17, La Latina.**
Tel: 91 366 4217
Open: 1–4pm, 8pm–midnight daily                    €38

If you don't mind squeezing in with hordes of eager tourists, check out this restaurant, famous for its listing in the *Guinness Book of Records* as the world's oldest restaurant. It dates back to 1725 and is a four-storey rambling den with narrow staircases, exposed beams and partly tiled walls. Each floor has its own atmosphere, but the basement is the most popular. The speciality is roast suckling pig, and if it's not too frantic (which it probably

will be) you might be able to persuade one of the helpful and pleasant waiters to show you the place where they're cooked. It's not a sight for the squeamish, however. This place is a landmark, which means that you are likely to be surrounded by those in search of an 'authentic' experience, but it's worth it nonetheless.

**Food 8, Service 9, Atmosphere 9**

**Brasserie de Lista, Serrano 110, Salamanca.**
Tel: 91 411 0867
Open: 1–4pm, 9pm–midnight daily                                €30

Smart businessmen and *senoras-that-do* gather at this restaurant at lunchtimes for *pintxos* at the bar. At night they all reconvene

to discuss the day's events in the formal brasserie restaurant. In the same street as most of the top designer stores, and surrounded by large finance houses and diplomatic residences, the Brasserie attracts Madrid's social elite. The food has a French slant, so expect rich sauces with everything and classic staple dishes such as *moules marinière* and grilled *chèvre*. There's a good-value three-course set dinner menu for €50 for two, including a bottle of wine or *cava*. To one side, there's a small covered terrace but heavy traffic and the odd irritating busker make it rather noisy.

**Food 7, Service 7, Atmosphere 6**

**La Broche, Calle de Miguel Angel 29, Chamberi.**
Tel: 91 399 3437
Open: 2–4pm, 9–11.30pm.
Closed Saturday lunch, Sunday and throughout August.          €45

The latest craze for minimalist, all-white interiors has reached new heights at this celebrated restaurant. Here, there is absolutely no trace of colour to be seen except, of course, for the delights that are served up on your plate. The radical and

somewhat surrealist work of chef Sergi Arola has earned La Broche two Michelin stars and given it a reputation for taking *haute cuisine* into new realms of creativity. This is food for the daring, especially when the menu features options such as loin of horse. Just off the Paseo de la Castellana, on the ground floor of the not-so-glamorous Hotel Miguel Angel, this is a popular spot for expense-accounted businesspeople and the Salamanca set. If you want to try modern Spanish cuisine at its very best, and don't mind tackling some intense combinations of flavours and ingredients, this is the place for you.

**Food 9, Service 9, Atmosphere 8**

**Café Oliver, Almirante 12, Chueca.**
Tel: 91 521 7379
Open: 8am–midnight, 1am Friday–Saturday.
Closed Sunday, Monday evening. €36

Famous for its Sunday brunch, Café Oliver is rarely quiet at any time. Enthusiasm for the restaurant is fuelled by the credentials of the owners, who've worked with the likes of Conran. The décor is simple but stylish, with a mixture of bare brick and painted walls, large mirrors, old-style advertisements and

exposed beams. The restaurant is on a corner and has windows on two sides, making it bright and cheery during the day. Friendly, good-looking and mostly English-speaking staff are dressed in black T-shirts and khaki aprons, adding to the overall

New York feel of the place. The menu is international, with a set lunch that changes daily. Pastas and risottos are served in miniature saucepans, keeping them piping hot, but the most popular dish is the steak tartar. You can't book for brunch, which normally consists of fried eggs, bacon and orange juice. Bookings are recommended at all other times. After dinner, head downstairs to EO, the restaurant's chilled bar (see page 108).

**Food 8, Service 9, Atmosphere 8**

**Casa Lucio, Cava Baja 35, La Latina.**
Tel: 91 365 3252
Open: 1–4pm, 9–11.30pm. Closed Saturday lunch.                    €40

A veritable institution, this is the place to come for traditional Madrileno food. It's heaving every night of the week, upstairs and down, and has proved a particularly popular spot for politicians, journalists and VIPs, and anyone celebrating a special occasion or hosting visitors from overseas. If you really want to do it properly, order the fried eggs on chips to start, following by suckling pig (and chips), and then rice pudding for dessert. It's certainly not short on cholesterol! Other specialities are tripe, oxtail stew, and green beans with partridge. Helpful waiters will talk you through the menu and keep your wine glass constantly filled with one of the great selection of Spanish wines. The setting is as traditional as the food, with exposed beams, low ceilings and leaded-light windows. Ask for a table on the first floor, where the atmosphere

is more intimate. This is normally a jacket-and-tie affair, but you won't be turned away if you are a little more casual.

**Food 8, Service 9, Atmosphere 9**

**Champagneria Gala, Calle Moratin 22, Centro.**
Tel: 91 429 2562 www.paellas-gala.com
Open: 1.30–5pm, 9pm–midnight/1am daily                    €16

After a morning of culture at the Prado, this is a great spot for a long, leisurely and siesta-inducing paella. From this restaurant's rather plain-looking and easy-to-miss frontage, you wouldn't guess there was a pretty glass atrium out the back where local families and the odd tourist tuck into huge pans of paella. The

set lunchtime menu is fantastic value and includes bread, pickled vegetables, salad (just a bowl of lettuce), a salsa and a garlic dip, a choice of paella and risotto, a pudding and a *porron* of *moscatel*. Go easy on the bread because the paella is huge and you won't want to leave any. The classic *negra* (with squid ink) is popular, but one word of advice – don't go for the *Madrilena con callos y sarbanzos* unless you're a big fan of tripe. English menus are available, credit cards are not accepted and there's only a choice of white or red house wine (€5 a bottle). It's not the best paella you'll ever eat, but it will certainly fill a hole before you move on to your next dose of culture.

**Food 6, Service 8, Atmosphere 7**

**La Chantarella, Calle de Luisa Fernanda 27, Malasana.**
Tel: 91 541 8003
Open: 1–5pm, 9pm–midnight.
Closed Saturday lunch and Sunday.                            €38

This tiny neighbourhood restaurant, run by brothers Enrique and
Alvaro Diaz, focuses clearly on the food, and when it's of such
high quality you can easily forgive the fact that the walls are

painted in rather tacky bright primary colours and the menus
look like they've seen better days. The judges at Madrid's Fusion
gastro-fair certainly did when they shortlisted La Chantarella for
Best Newcomer award in 2002. Instead of trying to be
original and wacky, the brothers stick to the robust basics, but
with a magic touch that keeps the locals coming back time and
time again. Reservations are sometimes necessary up to a week
in advance, although with only nine tables that's not
so surprising.

Food 9/10, Service 9, Atmosphere 7

**Cluny, Calle del Prado 15, Centro.**
Tel: 91 429 2838
Open: 1.30–4pm, 9–11.30pm.
Closed Sunday evening and Monday.                            €38

The name of this restaurant was inspired by a tapestry portraying the five senses that particularly impressed chef Juan Carlos Ramos in the Musée de Cluny in Paris. Ramos, who formerly

worked at the Café de Oriente (see Snack) and the restaurant of the Spanish parliament, has risen to the challenge of doing his own, imaginative cuisine at this small but exclusive restaurant. The otherwise blank walls are dotted with tapestries of medieval scenes. Soft up-lighting and jazzy background music create an intimate atmosphere, while the glass frontage is frosted so you won't feel too conspicuous at the window tables (even though that's why some come). Apart from the tapestries, the décor is modern and minimalist, and predominantly dark blue and deep yellow. Service is attentive and friendly, but the best is saved for the presentation of the food. Each dish is immaculately arranged on plates that come in all shapes, colours and sizes. The mainly Mediterranean dishes are imaginatively created with a mix of flavours and influences from Basque and Asian traditions.

**Food 8, Service 9, Atmosphere 7**

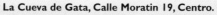

**La Cueva de Gata, Calle Moratin 19, Centro.**
Tel: 91 360 0943
Open: 12.30–4pm, 8.30–midnight. Closed Sunday.          €34

As its name ('The Cat Cave') suggests, this restaurant has two quirky touches – a huge modern print of a cat in the entrance and a downstairs eating area that's in a low-ceilinged, brick-walled room, just like – yes, you've guessed it – a cave. Now nearly 3 years old, this restaurant has earned a loyal following for its modern take on Spanish food. An imaginative menu, cosy atmosphere and a good central location have all helped its success. The menu changes four times a year, but there are perma-

nent flagship dishes, such as the caramelized endives with goat's cheese and the duck-liver pâté starters. The restaurant also houses exhibitions of work by local artists that change every two months or so. If one takes your fancy, you can buy it and take it home.

**Food 8, Service 8, Atmosphere 6**

**Le Dragon, Gil de Santibañez 2, Salamanca.**
Tel: 91 435 6669
Open: 1–4pm, 8.30pm–1am daily                                        €32

Remove the tables from this labyrinthine restaurant and it could easily be a nightclub. Spread over two floors, everything is fashionably black, except for huge red dragons painted on the ceiling and red and blue light-boxes scattered among the tables. Staff are highly efficient and courteous but seem a tiny bit hassled by the huge number of diners demanding their attention. The menu is crammed with traditional Chinese favourites, prepared in a lighter way so they don't leave you feeling bloated. Food can come at slightly irregular intervals but the flavours more than make up for this. This is indeed a beautiful place worthy of the attention of Salamanca's beautiful people – it is a little slice of intimate New York transported to a quiet corner of Madrid.

**Food 8, Service 8, Atmosphere 8**

**El Chaflan, Avenida de Pio XII 34, Chamartin.**
Tel: 91 350 6193 www.elchaflan.com
Open: 1.30–4.30pm, 9–11.30pm.
Closed Saturday lunch and Sunday.                    €45

It might be in a nondescript residential area, a bit of a trek from the heart of the city, and in the basement of a rather unglamorous three-star hotel, but this restaurant is regarded as one of the best in the Madrid. Chef Juan Pablo Felipe was the 2001 winner of Spain's National Prize for Gastronomy and specializes in cooking that isn't influenced by the current vogue for Asian fusions. Instead, he sticks to his Castillean roots with dishes such as chickpeas and chestnuts in ham soup and vegetable stew. The food is surprisingly light, so you'll still have room to try what El Chaflan is most famous for – its cheese board. Five different Spanish cheeses are laid out on a square plate, along with a variety of items, such as mini-biscuits and nuts, with which they are meant to be eaten. Unsurprisingly, this unique, stunning presentation of cheeses has won the restaurant awards. The spacious interior, painted in a pale silvery green, feels rather clinical by day but acquires a softer, more intimate atmosphere at night. It's definitely worth the taxi fare.

Food 9/10, Service 9, Atmosphere 8

**El Estragon Vegetariano, Plaza de la Paja 10, La Latina.**
Tel: 91 365 8982 www.guiadelocio.com/estragonvegetariano
Open: 1.30–4.30pm, 8pm–midnight (1am Friday–Saturday) €20

You're guaranteed good, hearty vegetarian food in a scenic setting at this La Latina restaurant. With its blue-and-white-checked tablecloths and ceramic tiled floors you could almost imagine you

had been whisked away to a tiny fishing village on the Spanish coast, especially as the view from the curtained window looks out over a quiet, leafy square. Trendy young things meet here at lunchtimes for the great-value set lunch, where portions are substantial enough to keep you going all afternoon. Mousakas, couscous and tasty soups are the mainstay, but the menu varies daily. There's internet access and even a non-smoking area, an almost unheard-of phenomenon in the Spanish capital.

Food 7, Service 7, Atmosphere 8

**Entre Suspiro Y Suspiro, Calle Canos de Peral 3, Centro.**
Tel: 91 542 0644
Open: 1–4pm, 9pm–midnight. Closed Saturday evening and
Sunday.                                                                           €42

This family-run Mexican restaurant, in a restored palace, is fun, romantic and stylish, all at the same time. Just off Plaza de Isabel II, home to metro Opera, it's a cut above the other rather

touristy joints in this area and certainly superior to the usual run-of-the-mill Tex-Mex. You won't find any sombreros hanging from the walls here. Instead, there are vibrant, modern paintings by Mexican artists (the owners themselves are painters). Lemons in huge wicker baskets sit on the floor around the bar, ready and waiting for repeated requests for pre- or post-dinner margaritas, and are also used to add some colourful decoration to the latticework dividing the dining areas. The food is elaborately presented Mexican *haute cuisine*, but portions are small so you'll probably want to order three courses here, especially after you've polished off all those margaritas.

**Food 8, Service 8, Atmosphere 9**

**Entretapas y Vinos, Calle Castello 24, Salamanca.**
Tel: 91 435 6333 www.entretapasyvinos.com
Open: 9am–12.30am Monday–Saturday; 9am–5pm Sunday    €28

This is one of a 17-strong chain of *tapas* bars/restaurants that are just right for a quick lunch to break up a shopping trip or

cultural excursion. They vary in shape and size, but all are designed with that sleek, industrial look that means plenty of chrome, and white and dark wood. The seating is mostly bench-style and you might find yourself having to share a table with others, but there are low-level wooden partitions for privacy. As the name suggests, wine is the theme and as well as plenty of bottles racked behind the bar, there are huge blown-up photos of corks and bottles on the walls. You might have to wait for a table, especially on weekdays when office staff flood in for their lunch break. It's a popular place for lone diners, but it's not a

good option if you want a leisurely, relaxing meal. It's geared
more towards a quick turnaround, so don't get too comfortable.

**Food 7, Service 7, Atmosphere 7**

### La Finca de Susana, Calle Arlaban 4, Centro.
Tel: 91 369 3557
Open: 1–4.30pm, 8.30pm–1.45am daily                      €17

Right in the centre of town, a minute's walk from the Gran Via,
queues begin to form as early as 1.30pm, and then again at 8pm
in the evening – a phenomenon almost unheard-of in the Spanish
capital. The reason? A ridiculously good-value set menu and
equally reasonable à la carte options, in a stylish setting. Here
the only problem is that you'll feel duty-bound to clear off the
moment you finish as a courtesy to the people still queuing.
Waiting staff, however, seem in no hurry to speed things along,
apart from the anxious-looking manager (he's the one you give
your name to when you arrive and who runs around like a head-
less chicken helping out with serving and keeping tabs on available tables). The set menu is only €6.96 (presumably this place

employed a strictly accurate conversion policy when the euro
kicked in), but includes three courses and a carafe of wine or
water. There's a choice of three starters and main courses and
two desserts. The à la carte menu has starters for around €5

and mains for €7, and the choice is enormous. There's even a section for those watching their figures. Fellow diners range from hip young students to coiffed old ladies. Whether you're on a budget or not, this place is worth the wait.

**Food 8, Service 8, Atmosphere 8**

### Indochina, Calle del Barquillo 10, Chueca.
Tel: 91 524 0318/0317
Open: 2–4.30pm, 9pm–midnight daily                €25

Sister to Tao sushi restaurant (see page 90), this modern, sleek Pan-Asian restaurant, close to the Banco d'Espana, is spread like a labyrinth over three floors. It's a favourite for business lunches and leisurely evening meals, and attracts a smart, cosmopolitan

clientele. The menu encompasses a wide range of styles, separated into dishes from Vietnam, China, Malaysia and Thailand. Attentive staff bring out trays laden with colourful Asian fare, all reasonably priced for such a stylish setting. There's a great-value lunchtime set menu that offers an interesting selection of starters, main courses, puddings and a glass of wine, beer, soft drink or water. The ground floor is where lunchtime business is done, but for an intimate meal head for the basement or first floor.

**Food 7, Service 9, Atmosphere 6**

**Iroco, Calle de Velazquez 18, Salamanca.**
Tel: 91 431 7381
Open: 1.30–4pm, 9pm–midnight daily                                    €36

Sometimes it's surprising which restaurants hit the spot and
which don't. There are plenty of restaurants equally as chic as
this in Madrid's exclusive Salamanca district, but for some reason
Iroco has become the place to be seen. The food isn't about to
win any awards, and there's nothing remotely Spanish about it –
hamburgers with bacon and cheese, pastas, salads. But this
restaurant still manages to attract Madrid's most well-heeled diners, dressed head-to-toe in Prada, dripping with jewels and
shrouded in that certain air that shouts 'money'. The décor is
modern with a touch of the Oriental, and out the back there's a

pretty private garden, but you'll have to book ahead to secure a
table here in the summer months.

**Food 7, Service 8, Atmosphere 8**

**La Isla del Tesoro, Manuela Malsana 3, Malasana.**
Tel 91 593 1440 www.isladeltesoro.net
Open: 1.30pm–1am daily                                               €28

One of a new generation of vegetarian restaurants in Madrid
(they've been slow to catch on in this ham-loving city), La Isla del
Tesoro serves healthy and tasty meals in an attractive, grotto-style
setting. Its name translates as 'The Treasure Island', and so naturally

the decoration adopts this theme. A fishing net hangs from the ceiling, adorned with fairy-lights, and a starfish hangs on the wall. An imaginative set-lunch menu is based on a different national cuisine each day – perhaps Greek, Indian, Moroccan, African or Spanish. It is great value and all dishes are designed to provide a complete and balanced meal. On the à la carte menu, the starters are almost the same price as main courses, but both are still reasonable. There's an English menu and descriptions of some of the ingredients, for those who aren't dedicated followers of all things

veggie. Unlike most, it doesn't close between lunch and dinner, so is popular for teas and snacks in the late afternoon.

**Food 8, Service 7, Atmosphere 8**

### Kikuyu, Bárbara de Braganza 4, Chueca.
Tel: 91 319 6611
Open: 1.30–3.45pm, 9.15pm–midnight. Closed Sunday.     €37

Simplicity and elegance are the watchwords here. Situated north of Chueca and east of Salamanca, this neighbourhood restaurant attracts the affluent locals time and time again. The dark, intimate room is the setting for some delicious Spanish/Mediterranean cuisine: *carpaccios*, paellas and delicate fish dishes entice clients in, while a well-considered selection of wines complements the subtle flavours of the food. At the front a stainless-steel bar welcomes the customer, who is then led to a darker middle room that is perfect for genteel conversations, while at the back is a further room with an occasional terrace. Kikuyu, as you might guess, was named after the Kenyan tribe, but the connection is somewhat tenuous as the owner fell in love with the name after watching *Out of Africa*. This is a real neighbourhood treat, and you

will need to book at weekends. It would be great to start off an evening having dinner up here before heading to some of Chueca's more sophisticated bars.

**Food 8, Service 8, Atmosphere 8**

**Larios Café, Silva 4, Centro.**
Tel: 91 541 9397 www.larioscafe.com
Open: 9pm–1am for food; bar and club open until
4/5.30am at weekends. €26

This is a chic, stylish, New-York style restaurant/bar/club where the rather unglamorous and mediocre Cuban food doesn't really match up. That said, it's cheap and there's not much you can do with the Cuban staples of chicken, rice and refried beans. Still, you're not really here for the food. The high-ceilinged restaurant/bar is something to be seen, dominated by a huge column of feathers encased in a glass pillar, and a montage of provocative fashion photos. No wonder this place is popular for premières, corporate events and fashion shoots. The immaculate waiting staff, dressed head-to-toe in black, are quick and helpful. The

79

clientele is a mix of suited Madrilenos and more casual tourists, but all of them unashamedly hip. There is live Latino music every night, except for Mondays. Saturday night is the busiest, when the city's fashion set arrive late for the club downstairs. Get a taxi to your next port of call, since this isn't the most salubrious section of the Gran Via.

**Food 5, Service 8, Atmosphere 9**

**Lhardy, Carrera de San Jeronimo 8, Centro.**
Tel: 91 521 3385 www.lhardy.com
Open: 1–3.30pm, 9–11.30pm. Closed Sunday evening.          €45

Another Madrid institution, this restaurant has hosted politicians, dignitaries and royalty in the same elegant and formal surround-

ings since it opened in 1839. It has managed to retain its status to this day, largely as a result of its signature dish, the *cocido madrileno*. It's Madrid's trademark stew, and was the everyday dish in the city's homes from the 17th until the mid-20th century. The type of meat used would vary depending on the family budget, and sometimes simply on what was available. Here, at Lhardy, you'll only get the best, of course. If you want a lighter bite to eat, downstairs there's a delightful and rather grand *tapas* bar and patisserie.

Food 9, Service 8, Atmosphere 8

**Luna Mulata, Calle Reina 4, Chueca.**
Tel: 91 522 1326 www.lunamalata.com
Open: 2–4pm, 9pm–midnight; bar/club open until 2.30am.
Closed Sunday.                                                                          €28

Just off the Gran Via, on the edge of the trendy, gay Chueca district, this relative newcomer is one of a new breed of more sophisticated venues appearing in this part of the city. It was opened in December 2002 by a forward-thinking group of friends, including a painter, a musician and an entrepreneur who owns the highly successful Café La Palma in Malasana (see page 142). There's live music most nights in the den-like club downstairs, which is helping to put this place on the map. The restaurant is modern Spanish – duck magret cooked in Andalucian wine is one speciality – and there's a great set-lunch menu.

During your meal, grab a programme to see what's happening for the rest of the month.

**Food 7, Service 8, Atmosphere 8**

**Matilda, Calle Puigcerda 14, Salamanca.**
Tel: 91 435 8937
Open: 1.30–4pm, 9pm–midnight daily                                    €40

True to its name, there's something delightfully feminine about this stylish restaurant, which is tucked away alongside some of Madrid's most exclusive shops in a pretty little side street. It's cool and modern, but its pink and purple furnishings and table settings, single-stem flowers in glass vases and brightly coloured luminous panel of photographs by Robert Garver give it a warmth and cosiness that could only be achieved with a woman's touch. Indeed, it was designed by one of the restaurant's owners, Dana Galiana, who has won acclaim in the design world for her unique style. Tilted mirrors make this miniature restaurant (a former coach house) appear more spacious, and it almost doubles in size in the summer when you can reserve a table on a small garden terrace out the front. The food is described as 'modern fusion' and more than pleases the fashionable Serrano crowd. A great place for lunch on a summer's day or for a romantic dinner year-round.

**Food 9, Service 9, Atmosphere 9**

**Montana, Lagasca 5, Salamanca.**
Tel: 91 435 9901
Open: 1.30–4pm, 8.30pm–2am. Closed Sunday.                    €36

Small but incredibly chic, this restaurant is managed by Erika
Feldmann and Ignacio Gonzalez, who are around most nights
making sure everything is running to perfection (which it invariably will be). With only 10 or so tables to cater for, the pair and
their staff manage to make you feel welcome and special, but
without being too obtrusive. There's a surprisingly informal and
cosy feel about the place, despite the glamorous clientele and
the minimalist, rather sterile décor. There's just one velvet red
curtain and one lone print; otherwise everything is whiter than
white. But you don't need visual distractions. You'll be too busy
enjoying the beautifully presented, delicious food. You can even
watch it being prepared in the open-fronted kitchen. Good, solid
Spanish dishes with a slight Oriental twist are created using only
the best produce, some of which comes from Erika and Ignacio's
farm near Toledo. You won't be disappointed.

Food 9, Service 9/10, Atmosphere 8

**Mumbai Massala, Calle Recoletos 14, Salamanca.**
Tel: 91 435 7194 www.mumbaimassala.com
Open: noon–4pm (1–4pm Friday–Sunday), 8pm–midnight    €37

It's unusual to find a decent Indian restaurant in Europe outside the UK, so this one will come as a pleasant surprise to anyone with a taste for all things spicy. The menu has all the old favourites, and not only will they match up to your local curry house back home, they'll probably taste even better. Here, you'll get fabulous succulent chicken breast and sauces that aren't as heavy and oily as you're used to, making the whole curry experience seem more healthy but just as tasty. The décor is refreshingly modern, but still retains that Indian touch. Hindu latticework, rainbow colours, gold and deep velvets create a theatrical, Bollywood feel, but all very tastefully and stylishly done. The restaurant is divided into several areas, all with a slightly different feel. There's also a small bar, where you can lie back on cushions and loosen your belt after a good feed. As with all good curry houses, they do take-away too.

**Food 9, Service 8, Atmosphere 7**

**La Musa, Manuela Malasana 18, Malasana.**
Tel: 91 448 7558
**Costanilla de San Andres, La Latina.**
Tel: 91 354 0255
Open: 9am–5pm, 7pm–12am (1am Thursday, 2am Friday); 1pm–2am Saturday; 1pm–1am Sunday          €18

The first La Musa was so hugely popular, it's no wonder they opened a second. At both, even on week nights, you will probably have to wait a short while for a table, but that's fine. Just add your name to the waiting list, sit at the bar and sip a glass of wine or a *cana* and tuck into the free olives, crisps and hot salsa potatoes. This way, you can watch the waiters pass by with the colourful plates of food and see what delights lie in store for you. It's difficult to choose, however, as everything looks tempt-

ing. Fried green tomatoes with goat's cheese and hot, creamy croquette potatoes with mince, sour cream and guacamole are just some of the tasty bites on the menu. The best solution, and one which you'll see most people opting for, is to go for one of the taster dishes to share (you can do the same with desserts too, which are equally wonderful). There's a sizzling meat platter or an all-encompassing degustation dish, attractively arranged on a huge, round plate. You won't know which to try first. If something in particular takes your fancy, you can order it as a main dish next time. The two restaurants have different menus, but the quality is excellent at both, and it's fabulous value for money. For a modern, creative take on *tapas*, this is the place. The Malasana venue is noisier and attracts a trendier, party crowd but the La Latina branch is larger and its art-nouveau interior is more conducive to a chilled-out evening. If you have the chance, give them both a try.

**Food 9, Service 8, Atmosphere 7/8**

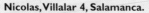

**Nicolas, Villalar 4, Salamanca.**
Tel: 91 575 1843/431 7737
Open: 1–4pm, 9pm–midnight.
Closed Sunday evening and August.                    €38

There's something reassuring about a hand-written menu. It makes you feel that the food is the most important thing here, and that you're in for some good old home cooking. At Nicolas, that's just what you'll get – hearty Spanish food such as pigeon, duck's liver, quails, chickpeas and stuffed cabbage – but all cooked so creatively that it cannot fail to please the most discerning diner. But don't expect typically Spanish-style décor. This restau-

rant is within the boundaries of swanky Salamanca, so there has to be a degree of modernity and minimalism. Thankfully Nicolas achieves this without being formal or cold. Low ceilings, low-level lighting and white linen tablecloths all do the trick. There is enormous attention to detail from the presentation of the dishes to the meticulously chosen wine list. It brings in a well-heeled crowd who love the serious cuisine and the attentions of the staff. Look out for Nicolas himself – he's the rather authorita-tive-looking chap who clearly knows his stuff.

**Food 9, Service 8, Atmosphere 7**

**Nilo, Calle de Jose Ortega y Gasset 8, Salamanca.**
Tel: 91 431 6060
Open: 1.30–5pm, 9pm–midnight daily                                    €34

This beautiful 19th-century residence, on one of the most prestigious streets in Salamanca, lends itself well to a restaurant conversion. The interior is refreshingly fun, with a mish-mash of designer furniture, leopard-skin throws and an assortment of kitsch chandeliers. Three dining rooms are separated by arches, the first room doubling as a bar/chill-out area dominated by a huge bowl holding magnums of champagne. Ceilings are wonder-

fully ornate and deep windows look out over the wide, tree-lined street. The menu is modern Spanish/Mediterranean and is surprisingly good value. Despite its exclusive location, there's no stuffiness here, and you're more likely to be sitting next to casually dressed models, celebrities and media types than smartly dressed businessmen and their lacquered-haired wives.

**Food 8, Service 9, Atmosphere 9**

**Nina, C Manuela Malasana 10, Malasana.**
Tel: 91 591 0046 www.ninarestaurante@telefonica.net
Open: 1.30–4pm, 8.30pm–12.30am (1am Saturday);
12.30am–5.30pm Sunday.                                               €28

This industrial, loft-style restaurant is more Manhattan than Malasana, which is a rather grungy and alternative part of the city. At any rate, it would be more at home in Madrid's swanky Salamanca district. Still, that doesn't stop it from attracting Madrid's affluent and style-conscious 30-something crowd, drawn to its high ceilings, bare brick walls and, of course, its huge selection of modern Mediterranean dishes. Only 2 years old, this restaurant has become famous for its Sunday brunches, but it's also packed at lunchtime and in the evening. The menu caters for most tastes, and offers six different soups. If you're lucky, you might even see the flamboyant and charismatic Nina herself. This is the latest venture for this Madrid entrepreneur who used to own Café del Foro, and now owns El Parnasillo next door (see page 105). The two couldn't be more different, but both are doing her proud.

**Food 8, Service 9, Atmosphere 8**

**Reche, Calle Don Ramon de la Cruz 49, Salamanca.**
Tel: 91 577 9379 www.Recherestaurant@terra.es
Open: 1.30–3.45pm, 9.30–11.45pm. Closed Sunday and
throughout August. €40

Another trendy, modern Spanish restaurant in Salamanca, but the décor here is a bit too clinical, with grey and shrimp-pink office-style chairs and white walls. It's L-shaped, and the best tables are in the lower part of the L – at the back, round to the left. Here you will have full view of the chefs through a glass window, all in

their whites, frantically chopping, stirring and adding the fancy, detailed touches to your risotto, steak or fish. The food is absolutely delicious and fabulously presented. Your fellow diners will be a mix of locals and those gourmets who have heard great things from their friends.

**Food 9, Service 8, Atmosphere 7**

**Santceloni, Hotel Hesperia, Paseo de la Castellana 57, Chamberi.**
Tel: 91 210 8840
Open: 12–4pm, 9–11pm.
Closed Saturday lunch, Sunday and throughout August.      €75

Madrid's reputation in the restaurant world went up a couple of notches when the Hotel Hesperia managed to secure the services of Santi Santamaria, famed for working his creative

genius at the *Reco de Can Fabes* in Sant Celoni, Barcelona. Here, at Santceloni (a name that even the Madrilenos struggle to pronounce), Santamaria uses the best local raw materials and, with attention to every intricate detail, mixes them together to conjure up delicious, first-rate dishes that quickly earned this restaurant its first Michelin star. If your wallet stretches that far, the best way to experience his genius is to opt for the 10-course Menu Gastronomique for €85 per person, accompanied by one of the new generation of Catalan wines that feature on the wine list (one of the best in the city). Designed by Pascua Ortega, the restaurant is ultra-stylish, set out with the usual neutral beiges, creams and whites, and provides the perfect setting for Madrid's high-society set, as well as those who simply love great food.

**Food 9/10, Service 9, Atmosphere 8**

**TAO, Paseo de la Castellana 45, Chamberi.**
Tel: 91 308 2780
Open: 1–4pm, 9pm–midnight daily                                   €38

Sister to Indochina (see page 76), this swish, slick sushi and *tepa-nyaki* restaurant is one of the most exclusive in the city. Since it's right on the Paseo de la Castellana and surrounded by luxury hotels, major banks and other smart office blocks, at lunchtimes it draws in well-groomed businessfolk, but is elegant enough to attract the more relaxed, leisurely, but still smartly dressed local crowd in the evenings. You'll find all the usual Japanese dishes on

the menu, and a surprisingly comprehensive wine list. A good option is to go for the set menus. For lunch, sit at the sushi bar and help yourself, but in the evening relax and let the charming staff do all the work.

**Food 8, Service 9, Atmosphere 8**

**Teatriz, Calle Hermosilla 15, Salamanca.**
Tel: 91 577 5379
Open: 1.30–4pm, 9pm–1am daily                                    €40

This converted theatre was designed by Philippe Starck and, in true Starck style, the lavatories are as much of a design feat as the actual restaurant, with huge, marble Louis XIV basins, and stainless steel and mirror cubicles. The circular restaurant is

dominated by a raised, gold-lit bar on the stage at one end, where moneyed Madrilenos and in-the-know out-of-towners gather for pre- and post-dinner drinks. Food is Mediterranean/Italian and surprisingly good value considering its Salamanca location and its Starck credentials. Service is efficient if a little abrupt, but that's all part of the exclusive appeal. English menus are available for those struggling with the language. Dress up in your best togs and treat yourself, and don't forget to check out the loos.

**Food 8, Service 6, Atmosphere 7**

**Thai Gardens, Jorge Juan 5, Salamanca.**
Tel: 91 577 8884 www.thaigardensgroup.com
Open: 2–4pm, 9pm–midnight daily                                    €32

There are several reasons why this huge, 350-cover restaurant manages to fill the majority of its tables most nights of the week. Firstly, there's its pretty Thai garden setting with lush palms, trickling water features and bamboo. Then, there's the excellent service. Dressed in traditional Thai outfits, the staff (mostly Thai, but also from China, the Philippines and other parts of Asia) are

courteous, efficient and greet you with a genuinely warm smile. Finally, there's the delicious Thai food, wonderfully presented and served in ample portions. Go easy on the melt-in-your-mouth prawn crackers and don't order too much. The menu has all the usual Thai staples, or plump for the set menu if you're particularly hungry. It's unlikely you'll be able to squeeze in the dessert, however. Ask for a table downstairs where it's cosier and the air-conditioning isn't as harsh, and if you really want the full Asian experience, there's a low table where you can lie back on cushions while you eat. This is as authentic a Thai as you'll get in Madrid, even though the owner is Chilean. He also owns Thai Gardens in Barcelona, Mexico, Casablanca and Paris.

**Food 8, Service 9/10, Atmosphere 7**

**La Viuda Blanca, Campomanes 6, Centro.**
Tel: 91 548 7529
Open: 1–4pm, 9pm–3am daily                                    €34

This über-cool newcomer has all the right ingredients to shake
up Madrid's restaurant/bar/club scene. La Viuda Blanca ('The
White Widow') is located in a quiet and elegant street just off
the main tourist route and two doors from the HH
Campomanes, one of Madrid's trendiest hotels (see page 36). Set
in a courtyard, with a dramatic glass roof, the venue was crying
out for a minimalist, industrial look, and that's just how it ended
up. It's all white, including the light-box flooring, apart from
orange cube candles on each table and a few scattered palms.
Taking the fashion for open kitchens to new extremes, this one
is completely exposed, with just a serving counter between chefs
and customers. Good-looking, mostly shaven-haired waiters
(apparently that's for hygiene as well as fashion reasons) wear
Hare Krishna style uniforms and glide around serving up creative
but not too fussy dishes and providing some eye-candy for the
girls. A DJ plays happy house from tiny decks and on the other
side of the bar there's La Viuda Negro (yes, 'The Black Widow'),
the bar/club where you can go afterwards for cocktails and flirt-
ing. The crowd is a funky 30-something, which provides a great
buzz. Definitely not to be missed.

**Food 8, Service 9, Atmosphere 9/10**

# drink...

There is no shortage of bars in Madrid, but as in any other major city you do need to know where to look. If you prefer to rub shoulders with in-the-know Madrilenos rather than fight your way through hordes of tourists, then you should be aware of the places to avoid.

There are plenty of bars on and around the Plaza Mayor, for example, but these tend to be over-priced and lacking in character, so the locals give them a wide berth.

Stroll over to the vicinity of Calle Echegaray and you'll begin to find a better class of drinking-hole. Beautifully tiled, traditional bars such as Viva Madrid and Los Gabrieles attract a good mix of locals and visitors and there's always a fun-filled and friendly atmosphere, while Ducados Café is a great spot to hang out at all times of the day and night.

Close by, three of the city's most famous and historical haunts, Museo Chicote, Del Diego and Bar Cock, are within a stone's throw of each other and have managed to retain their appeal over the years, while across the other side of the Gran Via, 1970s-style Suite has become the place to meet for a pre-club drink.

Cheuca, Madrid's colourful gay district, is home to some of the city's most fashionable bars, many of them just tiny, narrow rooms with basements that become hot and sweaty dance-floors at the weekend. The likes of El Clandestino, La Otra Habana and El Son, for example, might be small in size but are certainly big on atmosphere.

For more bohemian and laid-back venues, head to Malasana, one of Madrid's most up-and-coming areas. Although they might not look much from the outside, spots like Cafeina and Oui are super-cool hang-outs, while you're guaranteed interesting bar chat with the artsy crowd in Café del Foro and El Parnesillo.

The beautiful squares in La Latina are surrounded by fabulous *tapas* bars and cafés, many with outside terraces for warm evenings. Here, you'll find an older, sophisticated clientele, enjoying an *al fresco* glass of wine or a *cana* (a tiny measure of draught beer that's typical here).

Although drinking is a major part of life in Spain, long licensing hours, the *tapas* culture and a healthy attitude to alcohol means that it is consumed at a steady pace and therefore you are unlikely to encounter any trouble on a night out.

Thursdays and Fridays are probably the best nights to hit the town, but don't even bother heading out to a bar until 11.30pm or midnight. Some of the trendier venues won't start to fill up until closer to 1am when the clubbing crowd emerges for the long night ahead. Saturdays are also busy, but this is when younger, out-of-towners head into the city, so older, more discerning Madrilenos prefer to give it a miss.

The selection of bars listed here is a mix of traditional, funky and sophisticated, and all of them are within easy reach of the city centre. Remember, however, in Madrid there is a thin line between bar, café and restaurant, so many of the venues included in Eat and Snack also make a great place to have a drink.

**Areia, Calle Hortaleza 92, Chueca.**
Tel: 91 310 0307 www.aeriachillout.com
Open: 12.30pm–3am daily

For a totally chilled session, sink into one of the cushions at Areia, which bills itself as a 'colonial chill-out' bar. It's a bit of a loose description, however, as apart from the overhead fan it's more Arabian than colonial. The ceiling and walls are partly draped in red, there are colourful cushions everywhere, and there's even a bed tucked away in the far corner. A bohemian, studenty crowd gathers on Saturday afternoons to lounge around to ambient tunes. It's so dark inside, your eyes will need a few seconds to adjust. At night it takes on a whole new vibe, with DJs playing later in the week and on weekends.

**Balmoral, Hermosilla 10, Salamanca.**
Tel: 91 431 4133
Open: 12.30–3pm, 7pm–2am (2.30am Friday–Saturday)

Entirely different from any other bar in Madrid, Balmoral is smart but unstuffy and, with its grand fireplace and range of fine whiskies, you could almost imagine yourself in a remote castle in the Scottish highlands. It gets busy in two shifts – firstly from 7.30pm to 9pm with after-work drinkers or shoppers, and then with the up-market Salamanca regulars who arrive at 12.30 or 1am. However, passers-by are warmly welcomed and this is an ideal spot for a coffee or a last drink after a meal in one of Salamanca's smarter restaurants. The atmosphere is refined and civilized. There are no queues at the bar and no music, and plenty of chairs to go around. Balmoral first opened in 1955 and hasn't changed much since. In its heyday (in 1987/88) it was voted *Newsweek's* Best Bar in Europe.

**Bar Cock, Calle Reina 6, Chueca.**
Tel: 91 532 2826
Open: 7pm–3am. Closed Sunday (9pm–4am August).

During the post-Civil War period this venue served as a brothel and, although there are no such seedy dealings going on today, there's still an air of discretion about the place. The front door is locked and a doorman peeks through a heavy velvet curtain to see if you're worthy enough to be allowed entry. Inside, it's decorated

like a gentleman's club, with high ceilings and mahogany-effect furniture, and watched over by serious-looking (verging on snooty) bar staff. Moneyed Madrilenos sit back in embossed leather armchairs and talk politics, art or business. It's possible to reserve a table but you have to have some clout. In the old brothel days there was a tunnel that linked it to the Museo Chicote cocktail bar behind, but now you'll have to go the long way around.

**Bar Museo Los Gabrieles, Calle Echegaray 17, Centro.**
Tel: 91 429 6261
Open: 1pm–2.30am (3.30am Friday–Saturday, 11pm Sunday)

Inside this small, historic bar, which dates back to 1890, the walls are entirely covered in the most beautiful tiles and tiled pictures. Bar staff will tell you that there is an entire history behind each glazed tile and that Spain's finest flamenco dancers have performed before them. These days, there are flamenco shows every Monday and Tuesday starting at 10.30pm and again at midnight, but on other nights it's a mix of pop and rock. Somehow the likes of REM and Kylie don't sound quite right among the old pictures of bullfighting and posters of flamenco dancers, but this bar has chosen to cater for all. The crowd is a mixture of tourists (they're the ones staring at the walls in awe), and 20- and 30-something locals; go late in the afternoon, and you'll find families celebrating special occasions, or local businesspeople having a bite to eat. Drinks tend to almost double in price after 8pm.

### Café del Foro, Calle San Andres 38, Malasana.
Tel: 91 445 3752
Open: 7pm–3am daily

An older, more discerning Malasana crowd loves this quirky place, which is designed to look like a Spanish village. The main village square doubles as a stage, and in its time Café del Foro has been responsible for launching the careers of some of Spain's top performers. Today, it still puts on a varied programme of musicians, singers and entertainers, but with hot competition from other venues it doesn't attract the same high calibre of artists. However, even if there's nothing on, it's worth coming here for the décor alone. The atmosphere is relaxed and welcoming, and you're bound to meet some eccentric characters – that's all part of village life.

### Cafeina, Calle Pez 18, Malalsana.
Open: 3pm–2.30am. Closed Sunday.

Don't be put off by the rather shabby surroundings. This part of Malasana is in the midst of a revival that hasn't quite arrived. Cafeina is one of the bars that's helping to revive it, and from the numbers of revellers it attracts from Thursday to Saturday, it's doing a fine job. DJs play cool tunes from the balcony decks as Madrid's scruffy but stylish partygoers strut their stuff below. Downstairs a cave-like brick-walled room with low armchairs and minimal lighting creates a more chilled-out area. Cafeina is a good spot for an afternoon coffee, too, and then you can properly admire its deep purple walls, huge chandeliers and décor reminiscent of the Moulin Rouge.

**DeKonya, Don Pedro 6, La Latina.**
Tel: 91 366 3519
Open: 8pm–3am daily

When El Viajero closes at 1am, a young, hip, 'up-for-it' La Latina crowd heads here. The small, narrow bar/club fills up quickly, and soon the whole place erupts into a mass of dancing bodies, positively lapping up the energizing house tunes being expertly mixed by the DJ in the back room. Tuesdays, Thursdays and Fridays are the busiest nights. At these times, doormen are positioned by the

inconspicuous entrance and might give preference to regulars if the capacity is approaching maximum. There's no dress code as such, but the trendier you look the more likely you are to get in.

**Del Diego, Calle de la Reina 12, Chueca.**
Tel: 91 523 3106.
Open: 7pm–3am daily

You'll be spellbound by the skill and speed of the barmen in this tiny, low-key and refreshingly unpretentious cocktail bar. They look as though they've been mixing cocktails so long they could do it in their sleep, and while they're speedily crushing ice and adding salt or sugar, they will still be taking orders from whoever's next to walk through the door. There are 46 cocktails on the menu, all of them priced around €7. The house special, Del Diego – vodka, kirsch, peach, lemon and soda water – is a little disap-

pointing, however, so stick to your favourite. You can opt for table service at one of the few tables, but it's much more fun to stand at the bar if there's room. The décor is uninspiring but it doesn't matter – the cocktails take centre-stage.

**Delic, Costanilla de San Andres 14, La Latina.**
Tel: 91 364 5450
Open: 11am–midnight (2am Thursday–Saturday)

A cosy little café by day but a funky bar by night, this is a little gem among the many cafés and bars in La Latina. On summer evenings there's a pretty outdoor terrace on the beautiful Plaza de la Paja, but you have to arrive early to secure a seat. Inside, there are a few mosaicked tables and 1950s retro-style bar stools, but otherwise you'll have to settle with standing at the bar. It does get very crowded, but slope through to one of the back rooms and you'll be able to breathe more easily. Even if you're not hungry, you can't help but be tempted by the delicious home-made cakes on display, or one of the sandwiches, salads and *tapas* on the long menu. The staff are as laid-back as the customers, but that's what Madrid's café/bar culture is all about.

**Ducados Café, Plaza de Canalejas 3, Centro.**
Tel: 91 360 0089 www.ducados-cafe.com
Open: 8am–2am daily

This open-fronted café/bar is always heaving with people, day and night. Its interior is a lot of fun, with a strange but effective mix of black and white prints, huge pillars covered in newspaper print, plants, wicker chairs and a colourful mural at the far end. It is huge, but still has a warm and inviting atmosphere. Everything from pizzas and burgers to *tapas* and fried squid are on the menu. The price of drinks goes up after 11pm, and for some snacks you pay a fraction more at a table than you do at the bar. Breakfast is available until 12.30 and there's a choice of teas: English, Greek, Norwegian (salmon and tartare sandwiches),

French (lemon sponge cake) and more.

**El Barbu, Santiago 3, Centro.**
Tel: 91 542 5698 www.el-barbu.com
Open: 7pm-2am daily.

A labyrinth of a bar: you could hide away in here for hours and
feel totally cut off from the outside world. The further you go
inside, the darker it gets, and the more cave-like it feels. Bare
brick walls and spiral staircases are softly lit with neon pinks and
purple, and are decorated with drapes and pieces of fabric. Love-
struck couples take advantage of the dark corners and velvet
couches, while more sociable types sip cocktails at the bar.
Downstairs there's more of the same, with even more intimate
corners to explore. The place gets busier the later it gets.

**El Bonanno, Plaza del Humilladero 4, La Latina.**
Tel: 91 366 6886 www.elbonanno.com
Open: noon–2am daily

This lively, fun bar attracts a young and trendy, jeans-and-T-shirt crowd, who spill out onto the street most afternoons and evenings. Men stand around the horseshoe-shaped bar drinking beers and checking out the girls. It's the kind of place where everyone seems to know each other, and if they don't to start with, they soon will. The décor is bright red and cheery, with arty posters on the walls, and there's a rather novel way of distinguishing the men's from the women's lavatories (we'll let you work it out for yourself).

**El Clandestino, Calle Barquillo 34, Chueca.**
Tel: 91 521 5563
Open: 6.30pm–3am. Closed Sunday.

In the week it's a friendly, relaxed little bar where everyone seems to know each other, and where you might find the occasional live band playing. At the weekends El Clandestino becomes a shoulder-to-shoulder party zone, where enthusiastic DJs pump out house and hip-hop to a noisy, up-for-it crowd. If you want to let yourself go, head for the red-brick tunnel-like dance-floor, where everyone seems to be friends – or maybe that's just because they're squeezed in so tight. If you prefer to be able to hear yourself speak, stay upstairs at the ground-level bar, where the music doesn't distract from conversation.

**El Parnasillo, Calle San Andrés 33, Malasana.**
Tel: 91 447 0079
Open: 2.30pm–3am (3.30am Wednesday–Saturday)

Artists, journalists and intellectuals have been gathering here for highbrow conversation for years. Indeed, in the 1970s and 1980s the café was bombed by a far-right group for its part in the cultural revolution. These days, the clientele is still an interesting mix of colourful characters, including the flamboyant owner, Nina (if she's not busy with her newer venture, Nina, next door (see page 87). The art-nouveau décor, with floral prints, frescos and red velvet banquettes, lends itself well to the overall artsy feel. The bar staff are well trained and will quickly get to know your

favourite tipple, whether it's a cocktail or one of Parnasillo's famous alcoholic coffees.

**El Son, Calle Fernando VI, 21, Chueca.**
Tel: 91 319 5773
Open: 8am–2am (3am Saurday). Closed Sunday.

With no fewer than 90 different kinds on offer, this is a rum-lover's paradise. Work your way around the Caribbean and South America enjoying top tipples from Jamaica, Cuba, Venezuela, Barbados and Haiti and, when you're done, sober up a bit with a strong Colombian coffee. The music is naturally Latino and the atmosphere is incredibly friendly. However, the décor is surprisingly modern and minimalist – almost American diner style. Friendly bar staff will happily stop for a chat if it's not too frantic, and no doubt (after a rum or two) you'll soon be getting to know the regulars.

**El Tabernaculo, Plaza de los Carros 3, La Latina.**
Tel: 91 365 8542
Open: 10am–2am daily

One of the largest and liveliest bars in La Latina, El Tabernaculo is popular with overseas visitors and can happily accommodate large groups. It has an outside terrace with plenty more seating inside and a long, well-staffed bar so you shouldn't have to wait too long to be served. Neon lights change as the day progresses, creating different moods and atmospheres. The menu is all-encompassing and covers breakfast, lunch, dinner and snacks throughout the day, but grilled meats are the speciality. Check out the original Arabic wall to the right as you go in.

**El Viajero, Plaza de la Cebada 11, La Latina.**
Tel: 91 366 9064
Open: 1.30–4pm, 8.30pm–1am daily

Spread over three storeys, this place is everything in one – a restaurant, bar, lounge, pavement café and a garden roof terrace. Found on a corner a minute's walk from Metro La Latina, it's a natural meeting-place for the start of a night's bar-hopping. The ground floor restaurant is a little shabby-looking and serves mediocre food, but the huge first-floor bar/lounge area is a great place to settle into a chair and wait for friends to arrive. A few

cocktails later and you'll have probably decided to stay here until closing-time, especially if you've secured one of the more comfortable sofas. In the summer, the best spot is the roof terrace, for a buzzy atmosphere and fabulous views of San Francisco El Grande.

**EO, Almirante 12, Chueca.**
Tel: 91 521 7379
Open: 9pm–3am (4am Friday, 5am Saturday).
Closed Sunday and Monday.

In the tunnel basement of Café Oliver, one of Chueca's most fashionable restaurants, this bar has a ready-made clientele of pre- and post-dinner drinkers. However, it has established a loyal following in its own right, thanks to its classic surroundings, superb cocktails and funky vibes. Earlier in the week, you'll find elegantly dressed couples sipping champagne and making small-talk on suede couches, then from Thursday to Saturday DJs pick up the tempo with some choice tunes. Gorgeous-looking staff grace the bar at one end, expertly mixing cocktails and adding to the overall chic, up-market feel. Whether you're eating upstairs or not, this place is one for a special occasion.

**La Falsa Molestia, Calle Magdalena 32, Centro.**
Tel: 91 420 3238
Open: 5pm–3am Wednesday–Sunday. Closed August.

Hardcore clubbers gather here to rev themselves up for the night of partying ahead. It has recently undergone a refurbishment, but to look at it you wouldn't think so. Inside, it resembles a canteen in a student's union, with brightly painted walls and cheap-looking furniture. However, the main focus here is the music, which will soon get you out of your seat and into the fray. Regular DJ sessions attract a loyal following and the bar has become the official venue for a drink before Friday nights at The Room (see page 149). Even the staff join in the party, but ask nicely and they'll stub out their roll-up and pop back behind the bar to mix you a cocktail.

**La Fontana de Oro, Calle Victoria I, Centro.**
Open: 11am–very late, daily

Dating back over 200 years, this place thankfully retained all of its old charm when it was transformed into an Irish pub. Its windows are lined with shelves of dusty bottles and its walls are covered in old portraits, mirrors and of course the good old Guinness sign. Street lamps add some soft light to the rather dark and dusky atmosphere. This place is hugely popular both with tourists and fun-loving locals, and becomes particularly raucous when live bands play Thursday to Saturday at around 11pm. Of course, there's a TV screen showing all the major sporting events, too, but it doesn't dominate the bar.

**Geografic Club, Calle Alcala 141, Salamanca.**
Tel: 91 578 0862
Open: 1pm–2am (3am Saturday)

There aren't many bars in Barrio Salamanca, let alone decent ones, so it's not surprising that the Geografic is packed day and night. It's a vast, three-storey space with an enormous and beautiful stained-glass doorway and skylight through which the sun seeps during the day. As the name suggests, the theme is colonial exploration, with posters and artefacts from the far corners of the world, including African masks, snow shoes and the first hot-air balloon to land on Spanish soil. The chic Salamanca crowd pours in after work, staying until later in the evening. There's a reasonably priced restaurant upstairs but most people are happy to munch on the *tapas* and snacks, such as fried vegetables and

deep-fried goat's cheese. The chocolate brownies are hugely popular with the late-night coffee crowd.

**Museo Chicote, Gran Via 12, Centro.**
Tel: 91 532 6737 www.museo-chicote.com
Open: 7.30am–3am daily

One of Madrid's most famous cocktail bars and once the hang-out of Hemingway, Ava Gardner, Grace Kelly and most of Spain's most famous writers, actors and artists. Today, it's still one of the coolest bars around. Its interior is authentic 1930s art deco, complete with a revolving door entrance and alcove seating. Believe it or not, the seats are original so when you sit yourself down just think who might have sat there before you. Once you've slung your jacket over the train-style overhead racks and secured yourself a table, you won't want to leave. Cocktails are slightly more expensive than in other Madrid bars, but it's worth it for the atmosphere. Pick up a flyer from the counter, which will tell you what live bands and DJs are performing throughout the month. Since it opens again at 7.30am, you can even go back for breakfast.

**Olivera, Calle Santo Tome 8, Chueca. (No telephone)**
Open: 9pm–2.30am daily

Pillars and red velvet drapes create an elegant look but lampshades and scattered armchairs make this bar warm and cosy. A

soft, yellow glow can be seen through the front window enticing in passers-by looking for a relaxed drink. Once you've settled into one of Olivera's cushioned sofas you won't want to move, except to stumble over to the bar, of course. There's even a piano, but it doesn't often get played. Instead the music is suitably chilled and ambient. The bar is run by Serbs and is named after Yugoslavian movie star Olivera Markovic, whose portrait dominates the room (she looks a bit like Catherine Zeta Jones). At weekends, the atmosphere is livelier but you are still guaranteed a chilled experience if you get here early and grab a comfy seat.

**La Otra Habana, Conde de Xiquena 2, Chueca.**
Tel: 91 522 7056
Open: 8pm–3.30am. Closed Sunday and Monday.

Perhaps one of the smallest bars in Madrid and nothing to get

excited about design-wise, but this place is an absolute must if you're a lover of Latin music. Once the margaritas and *mojitos* kick in, and the Latino rhythm takes over, everyone will be swinging their hips and swishing their feet well into the early hours. The lack of space means that some dancers will find themselves relegated to the small flight of stairs at the back, but that just doesn't seem to stop them. Even if you have two left feet, it won't matter here, as the super-friendly, unpretentious crowd will soon show you how it's done.

**Oui, Marques de Santa Ana 11, Malasana. (No telephone)**
Open: 10pm–3.30am Thursday–Saturday

Don't even bother getting to Oui before 1am, as the people who come are far too cool to be seen here any earlier. They're also too cool to dance, so there's no dance-floor as such, although as the night draws on you might see the occasional foot tapping or slender hips gyrating. This is where locals come to fill in time between going to a bar and a club, which is why it doesn't even open until 10pm. The bar stretches along two walls, lit by low-hung lanterns, while the other two walls are dotted with chairs and bar stools. It's very, very dark, but subdued neon lighting and

murals add a touch of colour. Dress glamorously and adopt an attitude, and you'll fit in fine.

**Stars Dance Café, Marques de Valdeiglasias 5, Chueca.**
**Tel: 91 522 2712**
Open: 1pm–2am (3am Thursday, 3.30am Friday);
5.30pm–3.30am Saturday

You'll find all types here (gay, straight, trendy, not-so-trendy, young and not-so-young) but all have one thing in common – they're out to have a good time. This bar/club is all things to all men. It's a café, restaurant and hang-out zone during the day and a great party venue by night. The food is mainly Italian, with fresh pastas and salads, but they also do a mean pancake. In the late hours, the fun moves to the basement, where DJs play house music to an eager audience. One of the most versatile venues in Chueca, Stars (as it is generally known) is a safe bet for a fun night out.

**Suite, Virgen de Los Peligros 4, Centro.**
Tel: 91 521 4031
Open: 1.30–5pm, 9.30pm–3.30am (4.30am Saturday)

This 1970s retro-style bar is a great spot for pre-club drink and, thanks to its central location just off the Gran Via, a popular meeting-place for young, trendy Madrilenos. If you get here first, grab one of the cream-coloured leather armchairs or sofas by the front window; otherwise, there are plenty of tables and chairs gracing this large space. The mixed but mainly hetero in-crowd shout above the house/trance/funk music that gets louder and harder as the night goes on. If you want to chat properly, out back there's a pretty garden terrace lit by fairy-lights. At lunchtimes and earlier in the evening these tables are reserved for those who are eating in Suite's restaurant, but later on you can just grab a drink here. If you want to dance, upstairs there's a smaller bar and dance-floor, complete with disco mirror balls.

**Viva Madrid, Calle Manuel Fernandez y Gonzalez 7, Centro.**
Tel: 91 429 3640 www.barvivamadrid.com
Open: 1pm–2am (3am Friday–Saturday)

One of Madrid's best-known bars, tucked away off the main drag but still heaving most nights. It's popular with ex-pats and over-seas students, as well as with locals who want to meet them. Everyone is soon tapping their feet to cheesy, commercial tunes that cannot fail to get people dancing. Upstairs tilted mirrors on each wall make the rooms appear bigger and mean that you can check out the talent without being noticed. Be prepared to fight your way to the bar at weekends, but if you're lucky you will have got there early and secured a table out front for a much more civilized experience. If you can't face the crowds, check this place out in the day so you can fully appreciate its tiled décor, romantic prints and vaulted ceiling.

# snack...

Once no more than a bowl of olives with a glass of wine, the range, quality and creativity of Spanish *tapas* have taken a quantum leap forward in recent years. Today, *tapas* have become so sophisticated that they can end up costing more than a full restaurant meal.

The *tapas* concept originates in Andalucia, where a slice of ham or *chorizo* was placed on a plate that was used to cover a glass of wine and keep out dust and flies. In the 19th century, it took on a new role as crafty tavern owners began to use it as a way of making their customers feel thirstier and therefore buy more drinks.

As the custom swept through the country, regional specialities began to emerge. The Andalucian *tapas* tends to be *mojana* (cured tuna) or sardines with dry *fino* sherry, while Galacian bars specialize in octopus, prawns and seafood with Ribeiro wine. Madrid is known for its *patatas bravas* – tripe, assorted offal and snails in hot sauce. However, with such a massive immigrant population, you will find all sorts of national snacks and regional variations, particularly Arab and Middle Eastern.

There are several ways that *tapas* are served. A *pincho*, or *pinchito*, is a small tit-bit, no more than a mouthful and often on a toothpick, while a *racion* is a small

plateful. These will usually be served with bread. A *tosta*, meanwhile, is a slice of toast with a topping, while a *bocadillo* is a portion in a roll or slice of French bread.

In some bars you will find standing-room only, while in others there will be a small number of tables. Orders are usually made at the bar and often there is a limited range of snacks on display in covered counters on the bar. Payment isn't usually expected until you leave, and amazingly the bar staff manage to keep tabs on what you've consumed.

The best *tapas* bars tend to get extremely busy in the evenings, so be prepared to wait to be served. The whole idea is to take it slowly, and order little by little, or to pass from bar to bar, enjoying a bite to eat at each one.

In the less up-market bars, it's common to throw paper napkins and toothpicks on the floor after consumption, but it's wise to watch what the locals are doing before you discard your rubbish in this way.

Alongside the traditional *tapas* bars, Madrid is heaving with cafés offering all kinds of snacks and refreshments. Often venues that are lively bars in the evening double up as relaxing spots for a bite to eat and a coffee during the day, so check out the Drink section in this guide as well.

Café culture is thriving here, from breakfast in the morning to a coffee late at night, and there's no better way to get a real feel for the city than settling into a chair in one of its cafés and doing what the locals do.

**Almendro 13, Almendro 13, La Latina.**
Tel: 91 365 4252
Open: 1–4pm, 7pm–midnight daily

This wood-panelled *tapas* bar has retained an air of historic Madrid since undergoing tasteful modernization. Unlike most *tapas* bars, where the *vino tinto* is the tipple of choice, here it's more usual to go for a white wine or a dry *fino* sherry, served from chilled black bottles. Just help yourself to a glass from one of the huge wall racks and place your orders through the hatch. Loyal regulars keep coming back here for the great *tapas*, especially the *roscas rellenas* (rolls of bread stuffed with meat) and the *huevos rotos sobre patatas* (eggs and chips).

**La Bardemcilla, Calle Augusto Figuera 47, Chueca.**
Tel: 91 521 4256
Open: 12.30–5pm, 8pm–1.30am.
Closed Saturday lunch and Sunday.

After a frantic morning's shopping in this street of shoe shops, where better to rest your weary feet than this quaint tapas bar? Get here early, though, if you don't want to wait for a table. There are plenty of tables out back, but try to avoid the 3pm *tapas* rush hour (although you can always sit at the bar). La Bardemcilla is more formal than most *tapas* bars and is an ideal venue for businessmen conducting meetings, but most fellow diners will be shoppers and the trendy Chueca clan. The menu has all the staple *tapas* options – croquettes, meat balls, *chorizos* – and they're charmingly presented and speedily served.

**Bluefish, San Andres 26, Malasana.**
Tel: 91 448 6765 www.bluefishspain.com
Open: 8pm–1am Monday–Friday; 2–5pm, 8pm-1am Saturday;
1–6pm Sunday

This unpretentious, rather tatty-looking bar/café is famous for its Sunday brunch. Every Sunday afternoon, young, alternative Madrilenos gather here to nurse their hangovers with freshly

squeezed orange juice, mugs of tea and coffee, pancakes, scrambled eggs, breakfast potatoes, and whatever other specials are on the menu. The venue consists of three small, narrow rooms and you might well have to wait for a table. It looks a little like a student canteen, but it's cosy enough to be comfortable.

**Café Acuarela, Calle Gravina 10, Chueca.**
Tel: 91 522 2143
Open: 3pm–3am daily (4am Friday–Saturday)

Pour your aromatic tea from a stainless-steel pot while the Virgin Mary watches over you at this cosy, grotto-like café. The statue of the Virgin Mary, standing portentously in one corner, is one of the more obscure items of decoration here. You'll also find tiger-print chairs, cherubs, twigs lit by twisted fairy-lights and black and white photos of somebody's ancestors. The overall effect is remarkably soothing and makes this café an ideal spot for an intimate tête-à-tête or a place to recover from the night

before. This place is hugely popular with the Chueca gay crowd, so you'll have to time it right to secure a table and there's little room for standing. It's open till 4am Fridays and Saturdays, when the tipple of choice is more likely to be a *caipirinha* than a cup of tea.

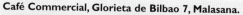

### Café Commercial, Glorieta de Bilbao 7, Malasana.
Tel: 91 521 5655
Open: 8am–1am (2am Friday–Saturday)

One of Madrid's most popular meeting-places, Café Commercial seems to be buzzing at all times of the day and night. In the summer, the prime seats are on the outside terrace where you can watch the world and his wife go by. Inside, there's a vast space full of tables. At one time, this would have been an elegant spot, but today this traditional café has lost much of its splendour. However, this hasn't stopped it drawing in the crowds. Although little has changed in other respects, the owners have brought the café some way into the 21st century by adding internet connections upstairs.

### Café de Circulo de Bellas Arts, Calle del Marques de Casa Rjera 2, Centro.
Open: 9am–1am (3am Friday–Saturday)

You have to pay €1 for the pleasure of sitting in this grand, ballroom-like café, situated in the magnificent historic building of Madrid's fine arts centre. It's a vast space, with plenty of seating, but you'll still be lucky to secure a table by the huge window. People from all walks of life sit smoking, chatting or reading newspapers while admiring the beautiful frescos on the ceiling, the enormous chandeliers, ornate pillars and larger-than-life naked statues. Highly professional waiters expertly balance coffees, wines and delicate snacks on trays as they dart in and out of the tables. This is perhaps one of the most relaxing places to while away the afternoon in the city and watch the hustle and bustle of life outside in Calle Alcala.

**Café de los Austrias, Plaza de Ramales 1, Centro.**
Tel: 91 559 8436
Open: 9am–1am daily

The owners of this large, old-fashioned café/bar/restaurant had to wait patiently for over a year while major construction work took place in the square opposite. Finally, in autumn 2003, they reopened to take over from where they left off. This traditional-style establishment is just across from Teatro Real and a 2-minute walk from the Palacio Real, and is a great alternative to the usual tourists' choice – Café de Oriente. It's simpler in style but still oozing charm and it's cheaper, too. In the summer there's an outside terrace and, now that the square has been renovated, it's an even prettier spot.

**Café del Espanol, Calle Principe 21, Centro.**
Tel: 91 410 4305
Open: 9.30am–3am Monday–Saturday; 9.30am–1.30am Sunday

You shouldn't have any trouble getting a table in this huge, high-ceilinged elegant café/bar, and even if you do there's still more space if you venture through the deep red-velvet curtained doorway at the back. Row upon row of marble tables stretch across the room while up above there are four giant green-glass chandeliers. It's right on the Plaza Santa Ana in the heart of the tourist district, but you'll find plenty of locals in here too.

Burgers and salads are served alongside a selection of more local fare, and a range of special coffees laced with whisky, amaretto and the like makes this a great spot for a nightcap.

**Café de Oriente, Plaza de Oriente 2, Centro.**
Tel: 91 541 3974
Open: 8.30am–1.30am Monday–Thursday, Sunday;
8.30am–2.30pm Friday–Saturday

Since it's right opposite the Palacio Real, in the pretty, leafy
pedestrianized Plaza de Oriente, you'd expect to find only
tourists here, but this spot is so good the locals love it too. This
elegant, traditional terrace café stands on the site of a former
monastery. Waiters are of the more mature kind and, despite
being a bit sour-faced, you can tell they know their stuff. Even
when every table is taken on the outside terrace (and there are
plenty of them), the waiters manage to keep on top of things.
Inside, the fake *belle epoque* décor, with mirrors, marble table
tops and candles, makes Café de Oriente a cosy spot even in the
chillier months.

**Café del Real, Plaza de Isabel II, Centro.**
Tel: 91 547 2124
Open: 9am–1am Monday–Thursday; 10am–3.30am
Friday–Saturday; 10am–midnight Sunday

Right on the Plaza de Isabel II, home of Metro Opera, there are
always people coming and going from this cute, unpretentious lit
tle place. There's a pizzeria downstairs but don't bother because

you'll find better pizzas elsewhere. Instead, stay upstairs in the cosy little café/bar area, or nab a table on the tiny terrace outside (you'll have to go downstairs to get to it) and enjoy a tasty breakfast, lunch or snack. The Teatro Real is right across the square, so if you're going to watch a performance pop in here afterwards for a coffee or something stronger.

**Café Gijon, Paseo de Recoletos 21, Chueca.**
Tel: 91 521 5425
Open: 7.30am–1.30am (2am Friday–Saturday)

Classified as a literary monument, this famous *tertulia* has been a meeting-place for artists and intellectuals since 1898 and, to this

day, still sponsors an annual award for new writers. Its friendly, grey-haired waiters seem to love their job and seem to feel a real sense of pride to be working in such a prestigious establishment. It's right on the busy Paseo de Recoletos, but once you're inside you won't notice the noise of the traffic. This is a great spot for an Irish coffee after a night at one of Salamanca's top restaurants, but is open for food and drink at all times of the day. A suited business crowd comes here for lunch on weekdays, but at other times you'll find all sorts. Definitely not to be missed.

### Café Mama Ines, Calle Hortaleza 22, Chueca.
Tel: 91 523 2323 www.mamaines.com
Open: 10am–2am (3am Friday–Saturday)

If you want to grab a bite to eat and read a newspaper while you wait for Chueca's funky shops to reopen, take a break at this civilized little café. It attracts a predominantly gay crowd, as you'll see from the various flyers and brochures on the table by the entrance. Flowery chairs and soft pastel-painted walls are livened up with modern art by local artists. Mama Ines serves six different types of breakfast until midday, followed by sandwiches and delicious tarts and pastries. Typical of the area, the café is right at home among the interesting and alternative shops which line this busy street. At night things liven up a bit, particularly at the weekend when it often fills to bursting point.

### Café Vergara, Calle de Vergara 1, Centro.
Tel: 91 559 1172
Open: 7.30am–midnight (2am Saturday–Sunday)

An opulent, traditional café right in the heart of theatreland, Vergara is popular with the arty crowd. Its cushioned banquettes, gold-painted chandeliers, gilded cherubs and pretty framed portraits all add to its charm. People come here for breakfast croissants and lunchtime *tortillas*, but mainly for the delicious cheesecakes and pastries in the afternoon. Smartly dressed staff stand ready for action and will do their best to please.

### La Carpanta, Calle Almendro 22, La Latina.
Tel: 91 366 5783
Open: 6.30pm–1.30am Monday; 11am–1.30am Wednesday–Sunday (2.30am Friday–Saturday)

This stylish *tapas* bar/restaurant is always bursting with people who come here for the lively, friendly atmosphere, its selection of over 50 wines, the fabulous food and a chance to gawp at the rather stunning-looking staff. La Carpanta is run by a family of Madrileno actors who have tastefully furnished it with quirky wooden furniture and flowery window boxes. Apart from that, it's just bare brick walls and wooden floors. If you want to secure one of the tables in the back rooms, add your name to

the waiting-list and join the throngs in the front bar. Thursday to Saturday you might have to wait up to an hour, but it's worth it (especially for the meatballs).

**Casa Labra, Calle Tetuan 12, Centro.**
Tel: 91 531 0081
Open: 9.30am–3.30pm, 8–11pm daily

Just off Sol, in the middle of Madrid's hectic 'high-street' shopping district, sits this legendary bar. The birthplace of the Spanish Socialist Party in 1879, Casa Labra has lots of charm – if you're prepared to overlook the slow, po-faced waiting staff (who look ready for retirement and seem to begrudge your every request) and the rather drab look of the place. As well as its historical significance, it's known for its *bacalao* (cod in fried batter) and *croquetas* (creamy croquette potatoes), which are served from the small, original zinc counter in the front room.

**Chocolateria San Gines, Pasadizo de San Gines 5, Centro.**
Tel: 91 365 6546
Open: 6pm–7am daily

Even those with a sweet tooth might find it difficult to get through one of the *chocolate con churros* that this place is famous for. The idea is to dunk deep-fried batter sticks into a cup of thick, sickly sweet hot chocolate – and you're supposed to do this in the early hours of the morning after a big night on the tiles. That's the tradition, anyway, and it's what Madrilenos have been doing since 1894. Today, this Madrid institution is full of sweaty clubbers from 4am to sunrise while at most other times you're more likely to find tourists snapping away with their cameras.

**Delic, Costanilla de San Andres 14, La Latina.**
Tel: 91 364 5450
Open: 11am–2am (2.30am Friday–Saturday); 9pm–2am Monday

A cosy café by day but a funky bar by night, this is a little gem among the many cafés and bars in La Latina. On summer evenings, there's a pretty outdoor terrace on the beautiful Plaza de la Paja, but you have to get here early to secure a seat. Inside, there are a few mosaic tables and 1950s retro-style bar stools, but otherwise you'll have to settle with standing at the bar. It gets very crowded, but slope through to one of the back rooms and you'll be able to breathe more easily. Even if you're not hungry, you can't help but be tempted by the delicious home-made cakes on display, or one of the sandwiches, salads and *tapas* on the long menu. The staff are as laid-back as the customers, but that's what café/bar culture is all about.

**El Tempranillo, Cava Baja 38, La Latina.**
Tel: 91 364 1532
Open: 1–4pm, 8pm–midnight daily

A well-stocked wine rack takes up one entire wall behind the bar and boasts impressive labels from all over Spain. Red wine or

*tinto* is the most popular choice with the sophisticated, thirty-something clientele, who love this rustic but classic place. Although a relative newcomer, El Temprannillo has already got a faithful following. The finest cured meats are carved at the bar and are served in large portions. It's mainly standing-room only, and tables are often reserved. The best seats, however, are the stools at the bar where you can watch the highly professional and rather serious-looking staff at work.

**Los Gatos, Calle Jesus 2, Centro.**
Tel: 91 429 3067
Open: 12.30pm–2am daily

There's paraphernalia everywhere in this fun, down-to-earth *tapas* joint. You name it, it's either hanging on the walls or plonked in a corner. The more bizarre objects of decoration include a rather garish statue of a choir boy wearing sunglasses, an old motor bike, several glass-encased football shirts, a street lamp and a bull's head. The atmosphere is casual and lively, bordering on raucous in the evenings. Goodness knows what they put in the beer but everyone in here has a smile on their face. A tiny counter, crammed in among all the odd objects, displays the delights on offer. Behind this, staff pour *canas* by the dozen as the orders are shouted across. It's cheap, definitely cheerful and well worth a visit.

**Jose Luiz, Calle Serrano 89/91, Salamanca.**
Tel: 91 563 0958
Open: 9am–1am Monday–Saturday; noon–1am Sunday

Although it doesn't look particularly special, inside or out, you can tell by the clientele that this *tapas* restaurant is good. It's the first of a highly successful Spanish chain that dates back to the late 1950s. On its pavement terrace, distinguished-looking gentlemen smoke cigars while their (sometimes remarkably) younger female companions, dripping in gold, hide behind Gucci shades. Despite the noise of three lanes of traffic and an occasionally strong gust of wind that comes up around the corner, you'll be lucky to get an outside table here. Dainty sandwiches, canapés and generous portions of succulent meats and deliciously creamy cheeses make up for the rather snooty waiting staff and keep the moneyed Salamanca set coming back for more.

**Lamiak, Cava Baja 42, La Latina.**
Tel: 91 365 5212
Open: 10am–2am daily

Walk past this place on a warm summer's evening and you can't help but be tempted in by its bright, cheery, orange interior and the buzz of its trendy young patrons. It is open-fronted, so the noise of chatter and laughter, above the happy house music, seeps into the street outside. Although it's always busy, the friendly young staff make sure the service is quick enough to keep everyone happy. Take your pick from the snacks on display on the counter or choose from the menu. After a few *canas* or tumblers of wine you'll soon be making friends with La Latina locals, but make sure you leave a path for whoever is next to be tempted inside.

**Museo del Jamon, Carrera de San Jeronimo 6, Centro.**
Open: 9am–midnight Monday–Saturday;
10am–midnight Sunday

You will find branches of Museo del Jamon all over the city, but the largest one is here, just off Puerta del Sol. Literally hundreds

133

of legs of *jamon serrano* (cured ham) hang from the ceiling and around the huge central bar. It's heaven for ham-lovers, but hell for vegetarians. The best hams are the *jabugos* from the Sierra Morena, but they're pretty pricey. But it's not just ham that's sold here. Enormous criossants and pastries make for a great breakfast or afternoon snack, or try one of the fabulous cheeses. Provided you don't mind being surrounded by raw meat as you eat, the food here is top notch and you'll be eating like the locals. This is also a great place to stock up for a picnic.

**Salon del Prado, Calle del Prado 4, Centro.**
Tel: 91 429 3361
Open: 2pm–2am daily

This elegant and refined Parisian-style café is a great spot to rest your legs after a hard day's sightseeing. The sun only just creeps through under the deep blue blinds and is substituted by softly lit chandeliers and dim wall lights. Add to this the background music of classical or jazz piano and you've got the perfect setting for a relaxing post-prandial coffee or a refreshing ice cream. If you're lucky enough to get one of the velvet-seated booths, before you know it you'll have whiled away half the afternoon. There's a piano in the corner and there used to be a classical pianist on Thursday nights, but this tradition has unfortunately been abandoned. Prices go up after 7pm, and after 6pm on Sundays and public holidays.

**Stop Madrid, Calle Hortaleza 11, Chueca.**
Tel: 91 521 8887
Open: 12.30–4pm, 6pm–2am daily

This quaint and quirky little *tapas* bar was a former ham shop
and dates back to 1926. All the original fittings have been
retained, including the marble counter, while bottles (covered in
years of dust) sit on the shelves that line the huge windows.
Ham is still the speciality and is consumed by the plate-load by
groups of Chueca trendies and families. If you choose a dish with
garlic in it, be warned – it is not used sparingly. This place is
hugely popular with the local crowd so you'll be lucky to get a
table. If you do, you'll be tempted to stay tucked away in here all
afternoon.

**Taberna del Alabardero, Felipe V 6, Centro.**
Tel: 91 547 2577
Open: 1–4pm, 9pm–midnight daily

Just behind the Teatro Real, this is a quintessentially Spanish *tapas*
bar and restaurant. Simple café rooms at the front have marble
tables and deep red banquettes while at the back red and white
tablecloths and elegant place-settings play host to locals and
tourists alike. The selection of *tapas* is a cut above what is normally on offer, but this – and its prime location – are certainly

reflected somewhat in the price. The staff are charming and have a vague smattering of English to help you understand what you are actually going to order. This is *tapas* at its best.

● **La Taberna del Foro, Calle San Andres 38, Malasana.**
Tel: 91 445 3752
Open: noon–4pm, 6.30pm–midnight daily

This simple, unassuming little *tapas* bar has a loyal following of regulars who sit at the bar, chatting with the proprietor as he serves up *tapas* and *raciones* of tasty nibbles. It's in a rather shabby little street, but this doesn't matter. Its pretty blue and yellow tiled walls, original zinc bar and shuttered windows will make you feel like you're on the coast, in a friendly Spanish village. The *tapas* menu is surprisingly large and has all the usual favourites.

When you've had your fill, pay your bill then head next door to Café del Foro for some live entertainment.

**Taberna Maceira, Calle Jesus 7, Centro.**
Tel: 91 429 1584 (also Huertas 66)
Open: 1–4pm, 8.30pm–12.45am (1.15am Friday–Saturday)

This funky Galacian *tapas* bar is like none other in Madrid. Its walls are painted in splodges of green (almost like the work of a class of schoolchildren), but the result is very effective. Even the menus are a novelty, scrawled on round wooden artists' palettes. The cheery décor creates a relaxed mood and attracts Madrid's bohemian, arty set, who chatter away while traditional Galacian bagpipe music plays in the background. The speciality is octopus and everyone seems to be eating it, along with other favourites such as salted roasted peppers (totally addictive) and *patatas bravas*. Staff are casually dressed and work like mad to keep the food and drink coming. Don't miss this place, and there's an even bigger one in Las Huertas.

**La Timba, Lagasca 61, Salamanca.**
Tel: 91 576 0186
Open: 9am–midnight daily

This funky, modern little café/bar is a great spot for a bite to eat day or night. Tasty, healthy breakfasts, Spanish and international snacks and a good choice of wines make this a popular hang-out with the Salamanca set. Right in the heart of the designer shopping district, La Timba is surrounded by exclusive boutiques and big-name stores; you'll probably find yourself sitting alongside perfectly groomed *senoras-that-do*, giving their credit cards a well-earned rest between purchases. Colourful, contemporary works of art decorate the walls and, along with cheerful staff, make visiting La Timba a truly pleasant experience. You'll want to come back.

**La Trucha, Calle Manuel Fernandez y Gonzalez 3, Centro.**
Tel: 91 429 5833
Open: 12.30–4pm, 7.30pm–midnight daily

For authentic Andalucian *tapas*, try this well-known rustic restaurant right next door to Viva Madrid (see page 115). Plates of all shapes and sizes hang from its white-washed walls, alongside bunches of garlic and onions, while outside there's a tiny pavement terrace, usually reserved for people eating full meals rather than *tapas*. '*Trucha*' means 'trout', and fresh trout is the speciality, but that doesn't mean you shouldn't try the *pescaito frito* (fried fish) or *berenjena frito* (fried aubergines). Waiters are of the more mature kind and there seem to be dozens of them, all intent on giving top service to the mix of tourists and wealthy (sometimes celebrity) locals who come here.

# party...

Madrid is the ultimate party town, so don't expect to get much sleep.

Most clubs here don't even open till around midnight and won't get busy until closer to 3am. Once they get going, the drinking and dancing continues until the sun comes up, and if you still want to keep going there are places where the beats keep thumping all through the next day. Even on a Thursday night, when many Madrilenos have to get up for work the next day, the clubs are heaving until 5 or 6am, with people still queuing to get in.

While Thursdays, Fridays and Saturdays are the busiest nights, many city dwellers prefer to give clubs in the city centre a miss on Saturday nights, when they are often overrun by out-of-towners. Instead, they stick to smaller, underground venues in areas such as Chueca, Malasana and La Latina.

Drinks aren't cheap, but measures are always at least doubles (bar staff don't use optics here so they'll just pour, often filling half the glass). With such large measures, and long opening hours, there's no need to hurry your drinks as you might back home. Drinks here should be sipped and savoured and pacing yourself means you won't be staggering home before the party really begins.

Many clubs include a free drink in the entrance fee, which is usually around €12–15, although at some of the cooler underground venues entry is free.

As in all major cities, the club culture is closely linked to drug culture, but here there are few bag or pocket searches by doormen. Door policies depend on the venue. In all cases, it's best just to be patient and wait in line, even if it's clear that the doormen are only making you queue to make the place look more popular.

If you decide to give up and go elsewhere, Madrid is so compact that it won't take you long to find another place. Most of the action takes place within a one-mile radius, and if you are exploring the nightlife in districts such as Malasana, Chueca or La Latina, it seems that every other door leads to a bar or nightclub.

The largest, most commercial clubs are mostly in the Sol area and tend to be frequented by tourists or locals looking for tourists – just think back to the last time you went to a club in Leicester Square. The most exclusive are in the Salamanca area, where you'll have to dress accordingly, while the most fun are in Malasana and Chueca where the dress code is more relaxed and anything goes.

## NIGHTCLUBS

**Barnon, Santa Engracia 17, Justicia.**
Tel: 91 447 3887
Open: 11pm–6am daily

Funk, R&B and Caribbean tunes in an almost glamorous setting
attract a mix of celebrities, footballers and wannabes to this club,
just north of Chueca. According to the owners, the likes of Janet
Jackson and Will Smith have passed through. Most of the time,
however, Barnon is full of scantily clad *senoritas* and young, eager-
looking local boys. This club aspires to be more than it is, but it's
still a good choice for a lively, party atmosphere if you want to let
your hair down. Black Sundays here are particularly cool, with all
'black' music from rap to Latin to reggae. Watch your drinks,
though, as bar staff have a tendency to swipe any glasses that are
left unguarded, even those that are still full. When it gets really
packed downstairs, they open a balcony level but only let you in if
you're cool enough. Chances are you will be.

**Café la Palma, Calle la Palma 62, Malasana.**
Tel: 91 522 5031 www.cafelapalma.com
Open: 4pm–3am daily.

Be prepared for a bit of a squeeze at the weekends here.
Although the venue is by no means small by Madrid standards,

there's hardly room to breathe when the night gets going. The scruffy but hip Malasana crowd love this place for its unpretentious, anything-goes attitude. The décor is far from glamorous, but the atmosphere is lively and laid-back in a grungy, Malasana way. Live bands and up-and-coming DJs play here most nights, so check out one of the club's flyers for what's on. During the week, it's a bit hit-and-miss but worth going if you're in the vicinity and want a late night out.

**El Perro, Calle Puebla 14, Malasana.**
(No telephone)
Open: 10pm–4am. Closed Sunday and Monday.

This underground basement club is easy to miss. If it wasn't for the lone bouncer leaning on the door, you would never imagine

there was a club inside. A loyal following of dressed-down, trainer-clad Malasana types make this a happy, unpretentious night. It's funky and fun and more like a mate's party than a nightclub. And, like a mate's party, it's free, too. People are still arriving in twos and threes until well into the early hours and although the dance-floor ends up being a bit of a squeeze, there's usually room to spread out in the bar area. It's dark and cosy and the hours just fly by. DJs play a mix of funk, 1960s, 1970s and house, and know how to please the regular crowd. Young friendly bar staff seem to be having as good a time as the customers.

### Fortuny, Fortuny 34, Almagro.
Tel: 91 319 0588
Open: midnight–5am daily

With its beautiful leafy terrace, this is a terrific spot on a cool summer's evening. Sophisticated, professional 30-somethings come here for a civilized drink or two and then most jump in a cab and head down to Gabana. The terrace is a good size but inside it's cosier, with the tiniest of dance-floors (you're practically dancing with the DJ). Music is a mixture of dance, R&B and cheesy chart music, but dancing isn't a priority. Most people are happier chatting with friends at the bar or posing on the terrace. It's worth coming out this way if you want to avoid the younger crowd and if you want to be able to talk without shouting.

### Gabana 1800, Velézquez 6, Salamanca.
Tel: 91 576 0686
Open: midnight–6am Thursday–Saturday

Join the *Hola!* crowd at this exclusive Salamanca nightspot where
the queuing continues well into the early hours. The arrogant
doormen rudely ignore most newcomers, but will turn on the
charm as the regulars step out of their convertible sports cars.
However, grin and bear it and keep up an air of superiority and
you'll soon be in. Pretty much everyone here is gorgeous and
immaculately turned out (otherwise they wouldn't gain entry).
The few that aren't must have got here very early. The DJs play
mostly cheesy commercial tunes, catering for Spanish tastes, but
you probably won't be able to push your way onto the dance-
floor anyway. It's pretty dark – so, girls, if you want to get
noticed, wear something bright and glittery. You might even find
yourself in the Madrid society pages.

### Joy Madrid, Arenal 11, Centro.
Tel: 91 366 3733/35439
Open: 11.30pm–5.30am Monday–Thursday;
6.30pm–6.30am Friday–Sunday

Just off the Plaza Mayor, this converted theatre is particularly
popular with the American ex-pat crowd. The building's interior

is beautiful, retaining some of the original features of the 1872 theatre, but it's somehow too big and impersonal to create much of an atmosphere. It's still one of Madrid's most well-known night spots, however, and continues to draw in the crowds. The music is mainly pop and the crowd (apart from the Americans) is a mix of teenage locals, tourists (young and old) and expense-account executives who had one too many drinks at the business dinner and didn't want to go straight back to the hotel. It's not for serious clubbers, but fun for a bit of a boogie.

**Kapital, Calle Atocha 125, Centro.**
Tel: 91 420 2906
Open: midnight–6am Thursday–Saturday

This place bills itself as the king of all Madrid clubs, with seven floors, a cinema, a shop (selling Kapital T-shirts and mugs) and dance-floors to suit all tastes. In reality, however, it's not as vast as you might imagine, and some of its 'seven' floors are merely balconies. The main action is on the ground floor, where scantily clad dancers gyrate on the stage while a mix of tourists (mainly Brits and Scandinavians), ex-pats, stag and hen parties, and the locals who are usually not cool enough to get into other night-clubs dance badly below. It all makes for an entertaining experience and you certainly won't be short of new friends at the end of the night. To get a drink, you have to buy a ticket from a kiosk (located on each floor) and take it to the bar. The door policy is

surprisingly strict, considering the clientele, but wait patiently in line, be nice to the bouncers, and you'll get in eventually.

### Moma, Jose Abascal 56. (No telephone)
Open: midnight–late daily

A young, *pijo* crowd comes here for a pose and a bit of a boogie. It's one of those nightclubs that seems bigger than it actually is, thanks to a clever and sometimes confusing arrangement of mirrors. Raised platforms provide a good vantage-point for anyone on the pull (which seems to be most of the guys and almost as many of the girls). The door policy isn't strict but dress is generally smart and glamorous – guys in striped shirts and chinos and girls in black. The music is commercial house and disco and the dance-floor is packed. The word 'Moma' is emblazoned in red

lights wherever you look, in case you forget where you are! Come here if you want a glitzy nightclub experience and you can't get into Gabana.

**Pacha, Calle Barcelo 11, Chueca.**
Tel: 91 447 0128
Open: midnight–6am Thursday–Saturday

Beautiful rich kids and second-string celebs and VIPs come here for the glitz and glamour of this converted theatre, which has retained its original art-deco façade. It's one of the clubs that's managed not to lose favour with the Madrid crowd and queues swell well into triple figures on Thursdays and Fridays. The ultimate place to be, however, is in the VIP area on the far stage, but you'll have to get past the stern-faced security guys first. If you make it, you can lie back on one of the couches and check out the quality of the crowd below. The music is a mix of commercial pop and house, and the dance-floor is huge. Dress up and take lots of cash, and try to get to know someone with a VIP pass.

**Palacio Gaviria, Calle Arenal 9, Centro.**
Tel: 91 526 6069
Open: 10.30pm–2am Monday–Wednesday;
11pm–6am Thursday–Saturday; 8.30pm–2.30am Sunday

When this 19th-century palace was converted into a nightclub, the unimaginable happened. All the original ceiling frescos and other Baroque touches were retained, so when you come here it really is like attending a party at the palace. Once you've glided up the sweeping staircase entrance, you will find yourself in a labyrinth of rooms, each catering to a different crowd. Usually the Latino room is the most crammed but it depends on the night of the week. Where else can you chill out in the palace drawing room, or dance salsa in the grand dining room? Thursday nights are best avoided since it's 'International Night' and hundreds of young Spanish and foreign students and ex-pats wear badges indicating their home country and desperately try to make friends. The rest of the week, the crowd is as mixed as you'd find, but that's what makes this place special.

**The Room at Stella, Arlaban 7, Centro.**
www.theroomclub.com (No telephone)
Open: 1–7am Friday–Saturday

The Room is undoubtedly one of Madrid's coolest hang-outs, and shows no signs of falling out of favour with the city's super-trendy crowd. If you get there before 1.30am you probably won't need to queue, but things don't really get going until 3am. Then, the sunken glass dance-floor (complete with huge disco mirror balls) suddenly fills up with eager *fashionistas*, waving their hands like they just don't care to uplifting house and dance tracks. The overall look is 1960s retro, with psychedelic wallpaper and swirling projections. There are two long, well-staffed bars at either end and a small chill-out area, but few people are in a chilled-out mood. On Thursdays, the venue becomes 'Mondo', the music turns to funk and electronica, but the crowd remains just as energetic.

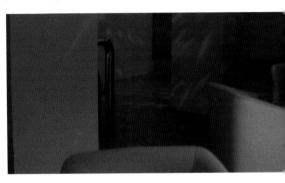

**Space of Sound at Macumba, Estacion de Chamartin.**
Tel: 90 249 9994
Open: noon–midnight Sunday

Ministry of Sound DJs pull in the crowds at this legendary Sunday session, when the place is bursting with serious, hardcore clubbers, some of them still sweating from the night before, while others are fresh-faced and raring to go. The best national and international DJs get things going from the start and make sure the energy levels don't die down until it's all over. The venue is enormous and when you need a rest you will find plenty of chill-out rooms with comfy chairs and sofas. Chances are, though, you'll soon be up again and in the thick of it. If you've made it this far, there's no point slacking now.

**La Vieja Estacion, Estacion de Atocha.**
Tel: 91 539 0679
Open: 10pm–2.30am Monday–Tuesday (3.30am Wednesday, 5am Thursday–Sunday), June–mid-September

A summer venue only, this vast terrace complex has no fewer than 10 bars, a restaurant, salsa rooms and an open-air dance-floor. The decorative scheme is Middle Eastern, with huge pyramid lights, pillars and wicker chair, with plenty of quiet corners for more intimate moments. It's right next to Atocha station, so it's handy for the bridge and tunnel crowd. The beautiful setting attracts an equally beautiful crowd and the door staff are refreshingly pleasant. The clientele is local and savvy and the outdoor venue puts everyone in a carefree holiday mood. There's a karaoke section, too, but don't let this put you off.

## MUSIC CLUBS

Flamenco has undergone a bit of a revival in recent years and there's probably no better place to experience it than in Madrid. However, don't expect the kind of performances you'll see in Spain's coastal resorts, with swirling red skirts and castanets. These displays are adapted for the tourists and are not a patch on the real thing, which is far more melancholy and emotional.

Here in Madrid, even in the venues that tend to cater for tourists, the flamenco is more authentic. Not all performances include dancing, but that doesn't make them any less moving or entertaining.

If you just want a taste of this Spanish tradition, some of the city's bars have occasional performances (Bar Museo Los Gabrieles, for example: see page 98), but for the top performers you'll have to book a table at one of the flamenco venues. They're expensive but worth it.

As well as great flamenco, Madrid is also home to a whole range of live music venues, including jazz and Latin. Look in the weekly *Guia del Ocio* for details of what's on where and when.

**Café de Chinitas, Calle Torija 7, Centro.**
Tel: 91 547 1502
Open: 9pm–2am (3am Friday–Saturday). Closed Sunday.
Performances start at 10.30pm.

One of the oldest clubs in the city, this is an expensive and somewhat touristy venue, but the performances are spectacular. If you come late, you can just pay an entrance fee and watch a show, but most people who come here go for the full formal dinner/dance experience. King Juan Carlos and Bill Clinton have both dined here.

**Las Carboneras, Plaza del Conde de Miranda, Centro.**
Tel: 91 542 8677
Open: 8.30pm–2am. Performances start at 10.30pm.

To see young, up-and-coming performers, choose this modern but cosy bar/restaurant. If you dine, you don't have to pay the admission charge and can choose from a selection of set menus. It's just as touristy as the others but the performances are particularly passionate and energetic, and the dancing is definitely the focus. The clientel tend to be younger and funkier here and the flamenco style does not necessarily strictly adhere to that found in more traditional establishments.

**Casa Patas, Calle Canizares 10.**
Tel: 91 369 0496
Open: 8pm–2am daily; performances at 10.30pm and midnight.

Reservations are essential here, since Casa Pastas hosts some of the finest performers you'll ever find. There is a restaurant for pre-performance dinners but it's rather expensive and there are plenty of better places to dine. Instead, call up and reserve a table for the late-night performances. The entrance fee includes your first drink and bar staff will serve you during the show, which is staged in a small and intimate room. At such close proximity, you can see every emotion in the faces of the musicians and dancers, and you can't help but be moved. Even grown men

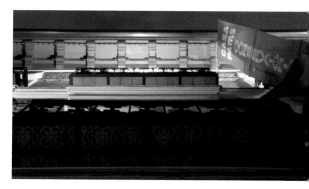

are regularly reduced to tears.

**Corral de la Moreria, Calle de la Moreria, La Latina.**
Tel: 91 365 8446/1137 www.corraldelamoreria.com
Open: 8.30pm–2am daily

Follow in the footsteps of Frank Sinatra and Ava Gardner and enjoy some top flamenco acts at this serious venue. You'll have to pay for such quality, however: the cost of food and drink is particularly steep, but the menu is really quite good. Originally opened in 1957, it has hosts some excellent shows, transporting the viewer back in time. Although it's touristy, it's not too showy so it feels more authentic.

**La Solea, Calle Cava Baja 27, La Latina.**
Tel: 91 365 3308
Open: 8.30pm–3am. Closed Sunday.

For a truly genuine flamenco experience, this is the place. It's like nothing you will have seen before or are likely to see again. Two tiny rooms are packed full of enthusiasts and gradually people start to sing or play guitar. Soon the whole place is wrapped in a swirl of emotion. It can be slightly intimidating at first but, with the help of a few drinks, you'll soon find yourself getting into the flamenco spirit. 'Visitors' are welcome, but you might find there's standing-room only.

## JAZZ

**Café Central, Plaza del Angel 10, Centro.**
Tel: 91 369 4143
Open: noon–1.30am (2.30am Friday–Saturday). Closed Sunday.

Once voted one of the world's top jazz venues by *Wire* maga-
zine, this art-deco café is definitely worth a visit if you're into all
things jazz. Varied programmes of local and international acts
perform in the elegant, high-ceilinged room. Top names, such as
George Adams, Don Pullen and Bob Sands, have all graced the
stage, alongside lesser-known but equally entertaining Spanish
acts. The atmosphere is laid-back and low-key, and you'll be close
enough to the stage to get the full jazz effect.

**Café Jazz Populart, Calle Huertas 22, Centro.**
Tel: 91 429 8407 www.populart.es
Open: 6pm–2.30am (3.30am Friday–Saturday).
Performances at 11pm and 12.30am.

This narrow bar hosts mostly jazz, but you might also get to see musicians playing blues, soul, Cuban, flamenco and even reggae. It's small and intimate and, centrally located among the bars and restaurants of Calle Huertas, it's always busy. It's advisable to get here early if you want to secure a good spot, close to the performers.

## ADULT ENTERTAINMENT

There are two main red-light districts in Madrid. One is centred around Calle Montera in the city centre and spills over onto the other side of the Gran Via. It's what you'll find in any other major city, with a plethora of strip joints, sex shops and bored-looking women swinging their handbags.

The laws surrounding prostitution in Spain are complicated. It's not illegal to pay for sex, or to solicit it, but it is against the law to pimp. In the past, the prostitutes working in the Calle Montera area have worked for themselves, are known to the police, and have been left to operate with little bother from the authorities.

In recent years, however, an increasing number of Madrid's prostitutes are coming from Africa, Latin America and Eastern Europe, and it has become obvious that these groups are largely controlled by mafias. Occasionally there are high-profile raids but largely these rackets carry on unrestricted. The influx from overseas has, however, swelled the industry and the authorities have taken the rather strange decision to move the prostitutes out of the centre and into Madrid's vast park, the Casa de Campo on the western edge of the city.

Along the main access roads that run through the park you'll find scantily clad women and transvestites lurking in the trees, waiting for passing traffic, day and night. If you take the Telerifico cable car across the park you will see them standing around, chatting to kerb crawlers. It doesn't seem to deter the Madrilenos from enjoying the park, however, and couples and families carry on with their picnics and afternoon walks undeterred.

### Oz Teatro, General Orgáz 17.
Tel: 91 572 0931 www.ozteatro.com
Open: 7pm–4am. Closed Sunday and Monday.

A large American-style table-dancing bar where very good-looking women strip on stage or on your table. Housed in an impressive old theatre, it is a cut above the back-street peep-shows and dancing clubs. Sophisticated and stylish… well, as much as a strip club can be. The complex houses a restaurant and bar as well as the club itself. In this department, the best that Madrid has to offer.

# culture...

The Prado is perhaps Madrid's most famous cultural landmark, home to some of the finest paintings in Europe. The works of Goya, Velázquez and Caravaggio grace the walls. It is a must for all those visiting the city for the first time.

Close by, but by no means less important, are the Thyssen and the Reina Sofia. The Thyssen is home to the collection of Baron Thyssen-Bornemisza, who put together a remarkable selection of Impressionist and Post-Impressionist art, housed in a beautiful palace that has been transformed into a contemporary hanging space.

The Reina Sofia houses one of Picasso's most famous works, *Guernica*, as well as some impressive pieces by Miró and many other works by 20th century artists.

Madrid's cultural life doesn't necessarily revolve around tramping through art galleries, since there are some beautiful parks to explore. The Retiro, home to wealthy Madrilenos, is more formal than the wilderness landscape of Casa de Campo and on a par with the stunning gardens of the Palacio Real. Madrid's public spaces and architecture are among the most breathtaking of any European city. Try to incorporate the Plaza Mayor and the Palacio Real on your tour of the city.

Madrid might not spring to mind as a leading capital for theatrical entertainment, but nevertheless it holds its own. The mixture of large, major venues and smaller, alternative ones means there is something to suit every taste.

Like the bigger art galleries, many of the theatres are closed on Mondays and most of the alternative venues are only open from Thursday to Sunday. As with everything else in Madrid, performances start late, at around 9–10pm, and at the weekends there are sometimes second, even later showings.

For programmes detailing what's on, get the local guide, *Guia del Ocio*, or look in the Friday listings in the daily newspapers.

Tickets range from €8 to €25 and are often cheaper on Mondays, Wednesdays and/or Sundays. They can be bought over the phone through La Caixa Catalunya (90 210 1212) and Caja de Madrid (90 248 8488), from El Corte Ingles (90 240 0222) or directly from the theatres themselves.

In October and November, Madrid plays host to the Festival de Otono, which attracts big international names from the world of theatre, while February brings the fringe festivals of theatre and dance – Escena Contemporanea and La Alternativa. Madrid's alternative theatre scene is tame in comparison to other cities, but it is flourishing, with venues opening up all around the city.

In the spring, you can enjoy dance performances of all kinds during the city's dance festival, Madrid en Danza. Although the main concert season runs from October to June, there are many open-air performances.

**Casa de Campo and the Telerifico, Paseo Pintor Rosales.**
Tel: 91 541 7450
Teleferico open: noon–8pm Monday–Friday, 11am–8.30pm
Saturday–Sunday, April–September

This huge, 4,500-acre woodland on the western side of the River Manzanares is home to the city's zoo, swimming pools, tennis courts, a boating lake, funfair and cafés. Once you stray from the main roads, it becomes pretty wild, with large stretches of woods and gullies. You'll only be able to cover a small part of it by foot, or even by bike, but take the Telerifico cable car from the edge to the middle and you'll get a better idea of the sheer size of this city wilderness. If you look carefully, you'll also spot the semi-clad prostitutes loitering among the trees and bushes (see page 156). Day and night, female and transvestite prostitutes parade their wares along the main roads, but don't deter the locals from enjoying their picnics or afternoon strolls.

**Centro de Arte Reina Sofia, Calle de Santa Isabel 52.**
Tel: 91 467 5062 www.museoreinasofia.mcu.es
Open: 10am–9pm (2.30pm Sunday). Closed Monday.

This huge exhibition space (formerly a hospital) houses contemporary Spanish art, 20th-century works from the Prado, and the Miró and Picasso legacies, including the famous *Guernica*. Its white walls, high ceilings and vast galleries are ideal for these modern and often large-scale works. The museum also has a theatre, cinema, library, restaurant and bar and from its top, fourth floor there are fabulous views across to Atocha station. Guided handsets in English are useful and cost €2.40.

**El Rastro, Calle Ribera de Curtidores, La Latina.**
Open: 8am–2pm, Sunday only

While most of Madrid is in quiet recovery from the night before, Sunday mornings in this part of the city get started early. Madrid's famous flea market is already filling up by 9am and by 11am it's positively heaving. At 2pm it seems as though the whole city has turned up to browse through stall upon stall sell-

ing clothes, jewellery, handbags, antiques and souvenirs of varying quality and price. It's not just about shopping, however. The Rastro is well worth a visit, even if you come away empty-handed. Be careful, however, because it's popular with the pickpockets and it's the tourists they target.

**Museo del Prado, Paseo del Prado, Centro.**
Tel: 91 330 2800 www.museeprado.mcu.es
Open: 9am–7pm (2pm Sunday). Closed Monday.

Known simply as the Prado, this museum houses one of the oldest and most important collections of art in the world. Two centuries of the finest works, collected by Spanish royalty, are shown in this magnificent building. You could easily spend several days here if you wanted to experience it to the full. However, if you've only got an afternoon you must see the works of Spanish artists Goya (especially his Black Paintings), Velázquez and El Greco. Don't bother with a guided tour but do invest in the €1 miniature books on selected artists, sold in little dispensers in the exhibition rooms. An electronic guide to many of the works is available in English.

**Museo Thyssen Bornemisza, Paseo del Prado 8, Centro.**
Tel: 91 369 0151 www.museothyssen.org
Open: 10am–7pm. Closed Monday.

Over 1,000 pieces of art, assembled by avid collector Baron Thyssen-Bornemisza, who died in April 2002, are on display in this neo-classical palace. Works span the 14th to the late 20th century and are mainly by European artists, including Degas, Manet, Cézanne, Van Gogh, Matisse, Picasso, Munch and Constable. Guides in English are available for €3.

● **Palacio Real, Calle Bailen, Centro.**
Tel: 91 542 0059
Open: 9.30am–5pm Monday–Saturday; 9.00am–2pm Sunday and public holidays.
Admission: free to EU passport-holders on Wednesday, otherwise €5.95 (€6.90 with a guided tour)

It took 26 years to build the splendid Palacio Real, and King

Felipe V, who commissioned it, was dead before it was finished. He chose the most prestigious architects of the day to build it on the site where the Moors built their original fortress overlooking the Manzanares River. There are 2,800 rooms in all (it was originally going to be four times bigger) but only 50 of them are open to the public. It's probably not worth having the guided tour, as there are plaques in each room explaining the key historical and architectural facts. The highlights are the grand Throne Room and the Porcelain Room, which is encrusted with 134 Oriental porcelain panels and silk hangings. Be sure to check out the views of the Casa de Campo from the central courtyard.

### Parque del Buen Retiro

No trip to Madrid would be complete without a stroll through the city's elegant El Retiro park, found just behind the Prado. Originally part of the palatial grounds of King Felipe IV (1621–65), they were opened to the public in 1868 after the ousting of Isabel II. Today, among its shady tree-lined avenues and around its artificial lake, you'll find couples, families, cyclists, joggers, buskers, fortune-tellers and drug dealers (not threatening), who come to rest in the shade, indulge in some people-watching, or just make a living. Sitting here for an hour can give you a perfect snapshot of how life is in the city and the people who inhabit it. All through the year, the park is central to city life and is full of people well after sunset, particularly on Sundays. Come and clear the head before a long Sunday lunch.

### Plaza de la Cibeles, Centro.

Despite being a major traffic junction, the intersection of the
Paseo del Prado and Calle de Alcala is also home to one of
Madrid's most famous and impressive monuments. The central
fountain depicts the Ancient Greek goddess of nature, Cybele,

drawn in a chariot by two lions. It is surrounded by some of the
city's most stunning buildings, including the 1904 Palacio de
Comunicaciones (perhaps the most elaborate post office you'll
ever see) and the 19th-century Banco de Espana. When Real
Madrid wins a big match, the fountain is boarded up in an effort
to protect it from raucous fans who like to celebrate here.

### Plaza Mayor, Centro.

This large, cobbled square was built in 1619 by Juan Gomez de
Mora as the town square. Positioned just outside the city walls, it
was used by medieval traders to peddle their wares without
incurring intra-mural taxation. The ceremonial centre of Madrid,
it was used for coronations, markets and bullfights. Today, there
are still plenty of shops in the elegant, arched arcades, some full
of tacky souvenirs but others selling fine local crafts. The square's
terrace cafés are packed with tourists (there's not a Madrileno in
sight), and on Sunday mornings it's transformed into a stamp and
coin collector's market. It's also home to one of the city's tourist
offices, although it's so small you'll be lucky to squeeze in.

165

**Plaza Oriente, Centro.**

One of Madrid's most beautiful squares, the Plaza Oriente has manicured gardens, statues, views of the Palacio Real and across the Casa de Campo. It was commissioned by Joseph Bonaparte, Napoleon's brother, and has a very French feel. The equestrian statue of Felipe IV and statues of ancient monarchs were supposed to adorn the royal palace but were thought too heavy. Just down from the park are the Campo del Moro gardens, which in medieval times were used for jousting tournaments. With their winding paths, neat flowerbeds and fountains the gardens make a lovely, civilized spot for a picnic or to read a book in the sun. The Cafe de Oriente, nearby, is a great place to enjoy a espresso overlooking the gardens.

## THEATRE AND OPERA

**Auditorio Nacional de Musica, Calle Principe de Vergara 146, Centro.**
Tel: 91 337 0100 www.auditorianacional.mcu.es

Although not the best-looking venue, this auditorium is hugely popular for its excellent acoustics and comfortable seating. It hosts one of Europe's top classical music festivals and is home to the Orquesta Nacional de Espana.

**Teatro Bellas Artes, Calle Marques de Casa Riera 2.**
Tel: 91 532 4437/360 5400 www.circulobellasartes.com

A stunning old theatre that stages some very good shows. More adventurous productions are shown at the Circulo, housed in the same building.

**Teatro Real, Plaza de Isabel II. Centro.**
Tel: 91 516 0600

Reopened after a €120 million and much-delayed renovation, Madrid's main opera and dance venue is finally making its mark. It's believed to be the most technically advanced theatre in Europe, and indeed the acoustics and effects are stunning, making the most of the top opera, ballet and musical performances now being shown here.

**Veranos de la Villa (various venues)**
www.munimadrid.es
July–mid September

The likes of B.B. King, Philip Glass, Caetano Velosos and Brian Ferry have graced the stage at the Centro Cultural Conde Duque during the summer months thanks to this partly council-funded festival. July is given over to rock, jazz, blues and Latin music while August brings flamenco and ballet.

# shop...

If the Madrilenos aren't eating or drinking in their spare time, they're invariably partaking in their other favourite pastime – shopping. In Madrid, looking good is paramount as much for men as for women, and wearing the latest fashion and the right designer labels means hitting the shops regularly, even in the hot summer months.

On the whole Madrilenos tend to dress pretty conservatively and it's common to see mothers and their young daughters, or fathers and sons, wearing similar-style clothes. But that doesn't mean that more funky, alternative fashion is not an option here.

There are several distinct shopping areas in the city, catering to different tastes and bank balances. For example, if you want designer stores and money is no object, head for Salamanca, where the likes of Gucci, Versace and Chanel sit side by side. If you're in search of a bargain, stick to the shopping streets around Sol with its predominance of high street fashion, think Oxford Street not Bond Street. While if you want something that is a little different and slightly edgy head into Chueca where the more bohemian and alternative shops are found.

No shopping trip to Madrid would be complete without a visit to its famous Sunday morning market, El Rastro (see page 161), although if you're familiar with London's Camden or Portobello Road, you might be disappointed.

Shops in the city centre open at around 9.30am and close as late as 8pm or 9pm Monday to Friday, although some smaller, independently owned shops will shut for three hours at 2pm. On Saturdays doors open slightly later at 10am and all but a handful of shops in the city centre stay closed all day on Sundays.

If you're short on time but want to treat yourself to some retail therapy, head for one of the Cortes Ingles department stores. Here you'll find high-quality fashion, homeware, accessories and pretty much everything else all under one roof (although sometimes stores are split across streets).

Good value high-street fashion chains Zara and Mango are dotted all over the city and are cheaper than in the UK. There's even a Zara seconds store on Gran Via where you can pick up T-shirts for no more than €8.

Sales usually run January–February and July–August. Be aware that if you are paying with a credit card, you will often be asked for photo ID, so carry your passport or driver's licence with you.

A small cul-de-sac that leads off the larger Calle Jorge Juan, this is the home to elegant Spanish designer shops which pull in the ladies who lunch of Salamanca. Having exhausted your credit card, pop down the road for a long lunch at Matilda.

**Alma Aguilar** Definitive fashion for the local ladies who lunch.
**Angela Navarro** Beauty products, facials and hairdressing for the smart set.
**Boxcalf** Ladies' fashion with elegant shoes and accessories.
**Gallery** Men's fashion from a range of top designers.
**Robert Clergerie** Divine French shoes.
**Roberto Torretty** Italian designer.
**Scooter** French clothes and accessories.

**Calle Jose Ortega Y Gasset, Salamanca.**

One of the premier shopping streets in Salamanca, Jose Ortega is home to some of fashion's smartest and most exclusive boutiques. Whether you want D&G or Versace, it's all here. And why not pop into Nilo for a well-earned lunch afterwards?

**Cartier** Beautiful jewellery and watches from this chic French house.

**Chanel** For that essential little black dress.
**Dior** Lives up to Salamanca's elegance.
**Dolce & Gabbana** Italian fashion at its finest.
**Escada** Simple but elegant.
**Kenzo** Essential male and female fashion for the discerning clothes-horse.
**Louis Vuitton** Fashion, luggage and accessories.
**Versace** The last word in opulent fashion.

**Calle Preciados and Calle Carmen, Centro.**

Just off Puerta del Sol, these two pedestrianized streets are dedicated to high-street names and smaller one-off shops selling cheap and moderately priced clothes, shoes and accessories.

There are three large branches of El Corte Ingles here and a large branch of Zara (although there is an even bigger one a short walk away in the Gran Via). Weave your way in and out of groups of teenage girls and tourists, and the occasional busker, and hunt out the bargains. Watch out for pickpockets, however, who regularly operate in this area.

**Area Real Madrid** Club superstore selling shirts and souvenirs at pretty hefty prices.

**Blanco** Funky and colourful women's wear, shoes and accessories at great low prices.

**Casa Jiminez** Gorgeous *mantonas* (Spanish shawls), *mantillas* (silk headscarves) and fans.

**El Cortes Ingles** Everything you'd expect from Spain's leading department store, but not cheap.

**O2** Glitzy costume jewellery and accessories.

**Sanatorio de Munecos** Old school toy shop with model cars, cuddly toys and dolls.

**Top Shop** Branch of the UK store but slightly more expensive than back home.

**Zara** Value-for-money fashion for men and women from this Spanish chain.

### Calle Serrano, Salamanca.

Madrid's smartest shopping street and home to all the top designer names, Calle Serrano is always heaving with traffic and

shoppers. Its up-market, air-conditioned shopping mall, Galería ABC Serrano, is a good spot for browsing on a hot day and boasts a fine selection of boutiques and some famous names. The well-known department store El Corte Inglés also has branches at numbers 47 and 52, although they are not as large as the stores on Calle Goya. More interesting boutiques are to be found on the streets surrounding Serrano, particularly Lagasca, Jorge Juan and Claudio Coello.

**Adolfo Dominguez** Collections of Spain's leading designers, both smart and understated.

**Alvarez Gomez** Simple, elegantly bottled fragrances, plus beautiful wash bags, hats and umbrellas.

**Centro de Anticuarios** Lagasca Gallery of Madrid's most reputable antique dealers.

**Christina Castaner** Designer *espadrilles* in all colours and styles.

**Concha Garcia** Contemporary and ethnic jewellery by top international designers.

**Lavinia** The largest and most stylish wine shop in Europe.

**Loewe** One of Spain's longest established fashion names, best for leather accessories.

**Mallorca** The main branch of Spain's best deli. Great for picnics and chocolates.

**Oilily** Wild, wacky and colourful clothes by this famous French name in children's wear.

**Oysho** Part of the Zara empire, selling sexy swimwear and lingerie.

**Purificacion Garcia** A sleek selection of clean-lined, minimalist clothes, bags and accessories.

**Santa** Gift-wrapped sweets and chocolates that are perfect gifts.

**Sybilla** Simple, stylish clothes (and homeware) in vibrant colours by the sorceress of Spanish design.

**Zara Home** Great-value homeware from this internationally known Spanish chain.

Madrid's gay district is brimming with small, trendy boutiques, mainly for men. Prices vary and there are some particularly good-value vintage stores and seconds shops selling designer clothes at discount prices. It's a great place to go for club-wear, and styles range from the plain T-shirt to the positively outrageous. In Chueca you'll find a plethora of shoe shops, particularly in Calle Augusto Figueroa, which is lined with one after another. Most shops close here between 2pm and 5pm, but there are plenty of cafés in which to while away the hours until opening time.

**Ararat** Three shops selling local and international designer clothes for clubbing and more formal occasions.
**Excrupulus Net** Funky and expensive shoes from Spanish designers Muxart and Looky.
**L'Habilleur** Discount designer wear and last season's leftovers at low prices.
**Jesus del Pozo** Chic women's clothing and *prêt-à-porter*.
**Matane** Funky clothes and accessories from European designers, collected by Austrian fashion-hunter Andreas Bogner.
**Pedro Morago** Jackets and stylish clothing for younger men.
**Piamonte** Handbags for all occasions, plus belts and jewellery.
**San Francisco Skate Farm** Snow-boarding gear that's wearable any time.

## Malasana

For grungy, alternative fashion and good-value club-wear, head to Malasana. There's no main shopping street so you'll have to explore its narrow streets and lanes to discover its little boutique stores and cafés. Most are independently owned and therefore close between 2pm and 5pm. Malasana also boasts some funky little record shops where you might pick up some rare imported labels.

**Ars 31** Ethnic-style accessories and homeware.
**Galeria Laura Marquez** Beautiful but funky jewellery by local designers.
**Level Records Shop** Knowledgeable staff and extensive collection of imported vinyl and CDs.
**Pena and Pegna** Ready-to-wear ladies' fashion and hats.
**Reiko** Asian-style homeware at reasonable prices.
**Shen Comics** Comic specialists with an Oriental focus.
**Snapo** Colourful and hip streetwear for serious clubbers.

# play...

With Madrid's summer temperatures soaring to the late 30s and the nightlife continuing well into the early hours, you might be tempted to pass your time here at a more leisurely pace. However, if you decide you want a more active break, the city has many sporting amenities. You only have to go to El Retiro park in the evenings to see that at least some Madrilenos are keen to keep fit. Joggers, cyclists, roller-bladers and speed-walkers mingle with those who prefer just to stroll or sit on benches soaking up the glory of the evening sunshine.

Madrid is home to one of the world's most famous football clubs. Since David Beckham's arrival at Real Madrid, there is even more of a reason to try to catch a game (and your other half will gladly join you, too!). Real's host of *galacticos* mean that getting hold of tickets can be pretty tricky, but you feel honour bound to try; failing that Madrid has two other excellent teams, Atletico and Rayo. For a really atmospheric encounter get hold of some tickets for the Atletico-Real derby.

Alternatively, why not take in a more traditionally Spanish event at Las Ventas bullfighting ring? Bullfighting has become a multi-million euro business and

employs around half a million Spaniards. Although this blood-letting will not appeal to some, a fight is actually an incredibly graceful experience with a ballet-ic interplay between matador and bull.

If being cooped up in a city is not quite your cup of tea, then feel free to explore the beautiful mountains that surround Madrid. One can hire a horse or a mountain bike, head out into the Sierra mountains and discover the natural fauna and flora or just enjoy some exhilarating thrills and spills. For those interested in field sports there are some fantastic opportunities to shoot par-tridge in the surrounding hills; these trips should be organized in advance from the UK.

Madrid is not a city known for spas and retreats; here we have found just two to recommend. The Chi Spa in Salamanca is perfect to book into for a massage after a hard day's shopping on Calle Serrano and its off-shoots. Alternatively try the Medina baths based on the traditional arabic concept of a hammam.

## BASKETBALL

Basketball is the second most popular sport in Madrid. There are two first-rate teams: Estudiantes and Real Madrid. The season runs from September to May and the best games are the play-offs from April onwards and the Torneo de Navidad at the end of December. Tickets cost from €5.

**Estudiantes, Palacio de Vistalegre.**
Tel: 91 422 0780/562 4022 www.clubestudiantes.com

Tall men in big shorts. The American game of choice has its influences in Spain. Tickets can be obtained through El Cortes Ingles (tel: 90 240 0222).

**Real Madrid, Pabellon Raimundo Saporta.**
www.realmadrid.com

They aren't quite as good as their footballing *compadres* but still enjoy a good scrap. Tickets can be obtained through the Caja Madrid ticket line (tel: 90 248 8488).

## BULLFIGHTING

In the last few years bullfighting has grown in popularity and has become more fashionable, despite opposition from animal welfare groups. It is not regarded as a sport, however. It is a theatrical experience rather than a competition between man and bull. To the Spanish, it is a celebration of death: having lived for at least four years on the country's finest pastures, the bull finally gets his 'day of glory'.

Top matadors are among the highest-paid entertainers in the world and can earn over €100,000 a day. The season lasts from March to October and times vary. Beer and soft drinks are sold inside and you can choose from seats in the sun or in the shade.

**Plaza de Toros de Las Ventas, Calle Alcala 237.**
Tel: 91 726 4800/356 2200 www.las-ventas.com
Open: 10am–2pm, 5–8pm Thursday–Sunday.
Closed November–February.

As this is probably the most impressive bullring in the world, with a 23,000 capacity, there's no better place to witness a bullfight; these are held every Sunday, usually at 7pm but sometimes at 5pm. During the Feria de San Isidro, from mid-May to early June, and the Feria de Otono, starting in late September, fights are held every day.

Tickets go on sale three days before each event, but tickets for the San Isidro are usually reserved long in advance by season-ticket holders. By law, 1,000 tickets must be held back to go on sale at 10am on the morning of the fight, but there are very long queues for these.

The following agents are worth a try for tickets, although they charge a 20% commission:
La Central (tel: 91 522 5946)
La Oreja de Oro (tel: 91 531 3366)
La Taurina (tel: 91 369 4756)

Front-row seats in the shade cost around €100, mid-range seats around €25 and gallery seats in the sun as little as €3.50. You can rent a cushion for extra comfort.

## CYCLING

Madrid is not a bike-friendly city, but it does have a number of parks ideal for a ride. The wilderness of the Casa de Campo is great for mountain biking, while El Retiro park is good for a short, easy ride. There are several companies in Madrid running mountain-bike excursions, mainly in the Sierra mountains, and if you're here on an extended stay you might want to go off for a two-night cycling break. Bicycles can be rented from:

**Bicicletas Chapinal, Calle Alcala 242.**
Tel: 91 404 1853
Open: 10am–1.30pm, 4.30–8pm Monday–Friday;
10am–2pm Saturday

**Bicimania, Calle Palencia 20, Cuatro Caminos, Tetuan.**
Tel: 91 533 1189
Open: 10.30am–2pm, 5–8.30pm daily

Excursions into the hills start at €5, which provides you with a
tour leader, insurance and snack. Longer trips are also good
value.

**Bravo Bike, Calle Montera 25–27.**
Tel: 91 640 1298 www.bravobike.com
Open: 10.30am–2pm, 4.30–8pm. Closed Saturday and Sunday.

Cycling tours with a touch of class: it includes accommodation in
luxury hotels and dining in top restaurants.

**Calmera, Calle Atocha 98.**
Tel: 91 527 7574
Open: 9.30am–1.30pm, 4.30–8pm. Closed Sunday.

**Esto es Madrid, Calle Torpedero Tucuman 18.**
Tel: 91 350 1160.
Open: 8am–3pm. Closed Saturday and Sunday.

As well as cycling trips, this company runs rafting and climbing
activities for young, adventurous types.

**Karakol, Calle Montera 32.**
Tel: 91 532 9073
Calle Tortosa 8. Tel: 91 539 9633 www.karakol.com
Open: 10am–2pm, 5.30–8.30pm Monday–Friday;
10.30am–2pm Saturday

Mountain-bike trips.

## FOOTBALL

There are actually three La Liga teams in Madrid. Atletico Madrid and Rayo Vallecano are lesser known, while Real Madrid is, of course, by far the most famous and popular. The season runs from September to June and league matches are usually played on Sundays at 5pm or 6pm. Tickets cost from €15 and usually go on sale a couple of days before a match, when massive queues form outside the box offices.

**Atletico Madrid, Estadio Vicente Calderon, Paseo de la Virgen del Puerto 67.**
Tel: 91 366 4707 www.clubatleticodemadrid.com

If you can, get tickets for the Atletico-Real derby – it is an intensely passionate affair. Forget Real Madrid-Barcelona – this is when the real handbags come out!

**Rayo Vallecano, Estadio de Maria Teresa Riverio, Avenida Payaso Fofo.**
Tel: 91 478 2253 www.rayovallecano.es

Although they have dropped out of La Liga in recent years, they are trying to fight their way back into the top flight.

**Real Madrid, Estadio Santiago Bernabeu, Avenida de Concha Espina.**
Tel: 91 398 4300/90 227 1708 www.realmadrid.com

Can anyone nowadays pay a trip to Madrid without feeling the lure of *los glacticos*, the possibility of watching some of the world's finest footballing talents in action? The only problem is that games take place on Sunday evening, so unless you book a very late flight it may mean a Monday morning off. Real Madrid has a telephone booking system through the bank Caja Madrid (tel: 90 232 4324), but you'll still have to queue to collect your tickets. The Bernabeu is Madrid's largest stadium, but although it holds up to 75,000 spectators, it is surprisingly easy to get in and out. It is best to go for the tickets that cost between €20 and €30 in the middle tier.

## GOLF

Seve Ballesteros and Sergio Garcia have put Spain firmly on the golfing map. There are some magnificent public and private courses dotted around the city which can get rather busy at weekends, so check ahead for availability.

**Club de Campo Villa de Madrid, Carretera de Castilla.**
Tel: 91 550 0840
Open: 8am–10pm daily

An expensive and difficult course. This club also boasts squash and tennis courts, clay pigeon and range shooting, hockey pitches, polo facilities, horse-riding and swimming.

**Olivar de la Hinojosa, Avenida de Dublin,**
**Campo de las Naciones.**
Tel: 91 721 1889
Open: 8.30am–8pm daily

A public facility. There are two courses, one 18-hole and one nine-hole, where rounds cost from €15.50 depending on how many holes you play.

**Parque Empresarial de la Moraleja**
Tel: 91 661 4444
Open: 10am–10.30pm Monday–Friday;
9am–10.30pm Saturday–Sunday

A nine-hole driving range just outside the city on the N-1 road to Burgos. Here you can play a round for €17 or pay €2 for a bucket of 25 balls on the driving range.

## HORSE-RIDING

Madrid is located on a dry plateau in the mountains of central
Spain, therefore if you do take time to get out of the city the
best and quickest way to explore the surrounding countryside is
on horseback.

**Indiana Parque Recreativo Natural,
Apdo Correos 32, San Martin de Valdeiglesias.**
Tel: 91 861 2799 www.indiana-sl.com
Open: 9am–8pm daily

Experienced riders can trek across rivers and up mountains.
There's also a school for beginners as well as a chance to try
climbing, archery and canoeing.

**Las Palomas, Club H'pico, Carretera de Colmenar Viefo.**
Tel: 90 872 8795/91 803 3176
Open: 10am–2pm and 5–7pm. Closed Monday.

Riding for all levels just a 30km drive from the city.

## MOTOR-RACING

**Circuito del Jarama, Carretera de Burgos,
San Sebastian de los Reyes.**
Tel: 91 657 0875

Motorcycling and truck-racing events are held here. This racing
circuit hosted the Spanish Grand Prix until 1992, when the event
switched to better-equipped circuits in Barcelona and Jerez de la
Frontera.

## SHOOTING

The red-legged partridge is a game bird that is noted for its
speed and movement. Guns from around the world descend on

Spain during the season (mid-September to the end of February) to try their luck. One can either dedicate a weekend to it or simply take a day out and enjoy the country air and the sport.

### The Partridge Club
Tel: (+44) 7000 868 935 www.partridgeclub.com

A British organization that lets out days that are surplus to their members' requirements. Located just over 30km south-east of Madrid, this private hunting estate specializes in high valleys and therefore some really testing birds.

### Shooting in Spain
Tel: 69 699 9173 www.shootinginspain.com

Partridge-shooting in two locations, one near Toledo and the other near Guadalajara; 20% are wild while the rest are put down each July. The company tries to guarantee you 600-bird days.

## SPAS

### Chi Spa, Conde de Aranda 6, Salamanca.
Tel: 91 578 1340 www.thechispa.com
Open: 10am–9pm Monday–Friday; 10am–6pm Saturday.
Closed Sunday.

One of Madrid's most chic spas, Chi opened in 2003 to much acclaim. This small and welcoming spa is in the heart of Salamanca; as you can guess from the name, it has an Oriental theme, and offers a host of treatments from facials to massages and full-body waxing for men. Slippers, bathrobes, towels and a private locker are provided, and consultants are on hand to advise on treatments. Cash tips are expected.

### Medina Mayrit Arabic Baths, Calle Atocha 14.
Tel: 90 233 3334
Open: 10am–noon, 2–4pm, 6–8pm daily

Located in a 100-year-old cistern just off the Plaza Mayor, these authentic Arabic baths offer 2-hour sessions throughout the day. Bathers can dip in and out of cold, warm and hot baths, and perhaps opt for a 15-minute massage as well. The baths are popular with couples and groups, and bookings are a must.

## SWIMMING

There are several open-air pools in Madrid, but unfortunately they close in September (even though temperatures can reach the early 30s for longer). Public pools each have their own pricing and ticket system and you might have to invest in a swimming cap to be allowed to swim in them. The most popular pools are in the Casa de Campo (see below) but there are also pools at:

Barrio del Pilar, C Monforte de Lemos (in the northern suburbs)
Tel: 91 314 7943
Canal del Isabel II, Avenida de las Islas Filipinas 54
Tel: 91 533 9642
La Elipa, Parque de la Elipa, Calle O'Donnell
Tel: 91 430 3511
Moratalez, Calle Valdebernado
Tel: 91 772 7100

**Hotel Emperador, Gran Via 53, Centro.**
Tel: 91 547 2800
Open: 11am–9pm daily, June–September

The roof-top pool at this hotel is open to non-guests for a fee of around €24. It has stunning city views and is a decent size.

**Piscinas Casa de Campo, Avda del Angel.**
Tel: 91 463 0050
Open: 10.30am–8pm daily, May–September

There are three open-air pools here, one Olympic-sized, one for children and one intermediate. They get very crowded at weekends but are fairly quiet during the week. At certain times they are closed

off for OAPs or particular activities (nude swimming for example!),
so it's best to call beforehand to make sure they are open. Facilities
also include changing-rooms, cafés and sunbathing areas. Topless sunbathing is allowed, and there is an informal gay area.

## TENNIS

Owing to the climate and a propensity for warm springs and
autumns, tennis is a popular sport in the Spanish capital. With
Carlos Moya and Juan Carlos Ferrero in the world's top 10,
Spain is riding high in the tennis world. Municipal *polideportivos*
can be rented by the hour, but you have to bring your own
equipment. Courts can be found at most of the city-run
swimming-pool complexes.

**Tenis Casa de Campo, Casa de Campo.**
Tel: 91 464 9167

This complex, close to the boating lake, has 15 courts and flood-
lighting. It's the best run public court and costs less than €5 for
an hour.

# Updates and notes...

# info...

## DANGERS

Pickpockets at the Rastro market and around Puerta del Sol are the biggest dangers in Madrid. Tourists are prime targets, so try not to look like one and keep a tight hold on your bags and cameras. If you are wandering the dark streets of Malasana, Chueca or La Latina in the early hours of the morning it always pays to be careful. Try and keep to the lighter, brighter streets or just grab a taxi.

## PUBLIC TRANSPORT

Madrid's metro is quick, clean, easy to navigate and ridiculously cheap. For a weekend stay, it's best to buy a ticket for 10 journeys (€5.20), which can be used on the metro and the buses. It doesn't matter how long the 10 journeys are – trips from the airport to the city centre cost the same as travelling just two stops down the line. Two people can share the ticket simply by passing it back when going through the ticket barriers. Each time the ticket passes through, a tiny mark is made on the back and the number of remaining journeys is displayed on the ticket barrier, so you can keep track of how many trips you have left to make. There is no collection of tickets as you exit the station. On some platforms, boards display how long it has been since the last train departed, while on others they show how long you will have to wait for the next.

## SMOKING

Smoking is a major pastime in Spain. Even in places where it is officially banned, for example the metro, people still smoke. Don't be surprised if you get a face full of smoke from a shopkeeper. It's unusual to find non-smoking areas in bars or restaurants, although bans in cinemas, theatres and on mainline trains are generally adhered to.

## TAXIS

Taxis are plentiful in Madrid (there are over 15,000) and you usually won't have to wait more than a couple of minutes for one. The only exception is when it's raining or late at night in the main bar and nightclub areas. You'll know if it's free if it has a '*Libre*' sign behind the windscreen and a green light on the roof. If the driver is also displaying a sign with a district written in red, this means he is on his way home and is not obliged to take you if it is not on his route. Taxi ranks are marked with a blue T. Drivers won't always speak English, but are generally good at knowing their way around. A taxi from the airport to the city centre will cost around €18–20 including a supplement. There are also small supplements for baggage and for trips on Sundays. Go to the official rank outside the arrivals area and ignore anyone who approaches you.

For a reputable taxi service, telephone: 91 371 2131; 91 404 1213; 91 547 8200; or 91 547 8500.

## TELEPHONES

All the telephone numbers in this guide are without the international code. To call from the UK, dial 00 34 before the Madrid code 91. Remember to have your international option activated on your mobile phone. Rates will vary.

## TIPPING

There are no hard and fast rules with tipping and locals tend to tip very little. However, visitors are generally expected to tip 5–10% to waiters in restaurants, and maybe to leave a few centimes in a bar. It's also customary to give small tips to hotel porters and lavatory attendants and to round up the fare or leave around 5% for taxi drivers.

# index

# index

# index